GETTING OUT OF SCALE-JAIL
FOR GUITAR

BY FRED SOKOLOW

With Editorial Assistance by Ronny S. Schiff

The Recording
Guitar and Vocals: Fred Sokolow
Sound Engineer: Michael Monagan
Recorded and Mixed at Sossity Sound

To access audio visit:
www.halleonard.com/mylibrary

"Enter Code"
4713-5306-9374-1020

ISBN 978-1-5400-2964-5

HAL•LEONARD®

Visit Hal Leonard Online at
www.halleonard.com

Contact us:
Hal Leonard
7777 West Bluemound Road
Milwaukee, WI 53213
Email: info@halleonard.com

In Europe, contact:
Hal Leonard Europe Limited
42 Wigmore Street
Marylebone, London, W1U 2RN
Email: info@halleonardeurope.com

In Australia, contact:
Hal Leonard Australia Pty. Ltd.
4 Lentara Court
Cheltenham, Victoria, 3192 Australia
Email: info@halleonard.com.au

CONTENTS

INTRODUCTION

If you play guitar, but have no clue how to make up solos—or if the only soloing device you know is the minor pentatonic scale, or blues box—you need this book!

Scales are useful tools for the soloing guitarist. A scale is like an alphabet; to say something, you take letters out of the alphabet to form words and phrases. Likewise, you form musical phrases from the notes of a scale, but if you just play up and down the scale or pick random notes, your solos aren't saying anything. Instead, they're bordering on musical gibberish.

If this describes your solo attempts, or if all your solos sound the same, you just might be stuck in *scale-jail*—but there is a way out.

First, to continue the language analogy, you need to learn to form meaningful phrases and melodies, instead of just running up and down a scale. Imitating the licks of excellent blues and rock players is a start; it's like developing a new vocabulary.

Second, to be a good soloist, you need to know where the notes are located so that *you're* playing the guitar, instead of the guitar playing you! Learning to play familiar melodies and embellish them is a first step in mastering this skill.

Finally, there are soloing strategies that are based on chords, instead of scales. Every accomplished lead player knows some of these techniques, whether they play rock, blues, R&B, country, jazz, or any other musical genre.

This book and the accompanying audio files will show you ways to form solos that express feelings and are musically meaningful. It's like a big chocolate cake, and if you keep eating it, you'll find the file hidden inside that will help you break out of scale-jail.

Let's get started!

Fred Sokolow

Fred Sokolow

JAILBREAK 1
What Is Soloing?

Before diving into soloing strategies, let's answer some basic questions.

First, what is a solo? We all know a solo is an *instrumental* section in a tune. Sometimes, it consists of playing one time around the chord changes, while at other times, it only lasts for a portion of the chord progression (a verse, chorus, or just a few bars of a verse or chorus). In other cases, solos are played over a whole new chord progression.

Now that we've defined a solo, what should it accomplish? In a vocal tune, an instrumental solo offers a break from the singing, so it adds variety. It can be a vehicle for displaying a player's virtuosity, or it can be an expression of deep emotion. Sometimes, it's both of those elements at once.

There are three types of solos:

1. You express the melody of the song and add some variations or ornamentation that allow you to have some fun with the basic melody. After all, they do call it "playing" guitar.

2. You disregard the given melody and create a new one that fits the chord progression—instant composition!

3. You combine both of these approaches, playing an ornamented melody for part of the solo and inventing a new melody for the rest of the solo.

However, it's important to note that before you can improvise a coherent solo that disregards the melody, you need to know *how* to play the melody. It's the same principle that mandates that in order to be a credible visual artist, you should know how to paint a nude, a still life, a portrait, and a landscape—a demonstrated mastery of your craft—before you choose to just splash paint on the canvas from across the room and call it art.

For this reason, to loosen the scale-jail shackles, the pages that follow will emphasize soloing that states or implies the melody. There will also be instruction on how to ornament a melody, plus the tools you need to play the other types of solos, in which you invent new melodies and really break free.

JAILBREAK 2
Solos Based on First-Position Chords

Let's start with an easy soloing strategy. If you are in scale-jail, or if you have no clue where to begin when it comes to soloing, this chapter will get you started in the right direction. It shows how to play solos based on chords—no scales involved. See? You're making your first steps towards getting out of scale-jail!

Good news for scale-prisoners: You can play excellent solos that are not based on scales at all! Instead, they can be based on the underlying chords, and that includes single-note or multi-note solos. Though there is very little attention paid to chord-based soloing in guitar literature, most accomplished lead guitarists are well aware of it, and many iconic solos of all genres are based on it.

To play chord-based solos, you follow a song's chord progression and make up melodies, licks, and phrases from the notes in and around each chord. This can be easy, even if you've never played a guitar solo in your life.

PLAYING THE NOTES IN EACH CHORD

One easy way to ad-lib, or improvise, solos is to make the chord changes as if you were picking or strumming accompaniment and randomly play single notes of each chord. This may not result in a brilliant solo, but if you vary the rhythm, it will sound coherent and will not clash with the song. It's a great way to get your feet wet playing chord-based solos.

The "Rock Ballad" solo that follows is an example of this strategy. The progression is similar to that of rock ballads like Neil Young's "Helpless" or Bob Dylan's "Knockin' on Heaven's Door." Listen to and play along with it, and then dial out the lead guitar track, playing along with the rhythm track while making up your own solos. Remember to actually finger each chord and execute every chord change that's notated.

 1. Rock Ballad

Here's another example. This solo is for a song almost everyone knows: "Take Me Out to the Ball Game." There is no scale that would fit all the chord changes in this tune, so a chord-based solo is required. Notice that the *phrasing* is varied. The song is in 6/8 time, and if you just played *arpeggios* (going up and down the notes of each chord), playing six notes per bar, it would be boring. Instead, this solo has phrasing similar to the song's melody, but any interesting timing would make for a credible solo, even though you're just playing the notes within each chord.

 2. "Take Me Out to the Ball Game"

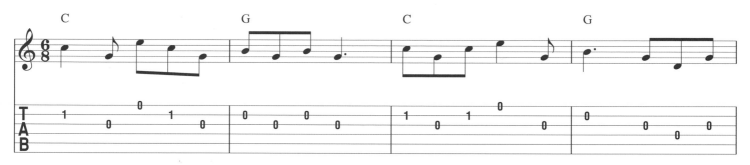

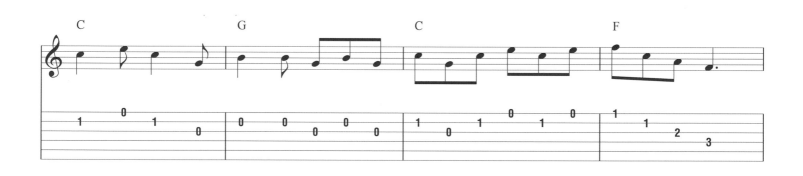

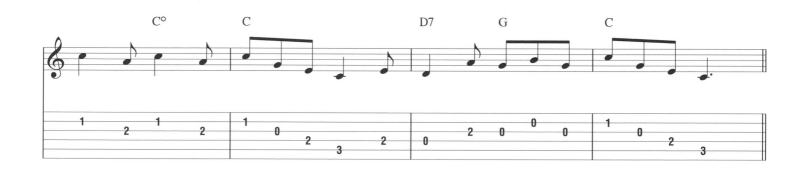

Here's another song most people know: "When the Saints Go Marching In." Once again, the solo consists entirely of notes of the chords. Notice how a good portion of the melody can be played using this easy method.

 3. "When the Saints Go Marching In"

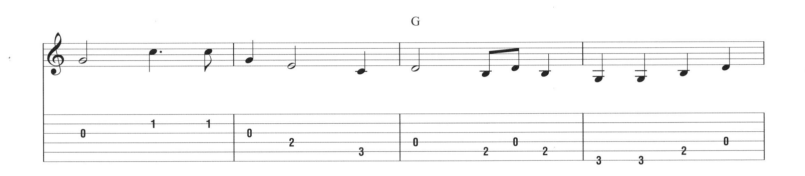

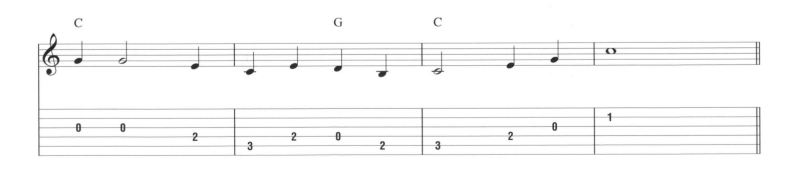

ADDING THE ADJACENT NOTES

While building chord-based solos, you needn't restrict yourselves to the notes within each chord—after all, you're not in *chord-jail*, either. Every chord you play has nearby harmonious notes that are useful in solos as well as discordant ones that are much less useful. Learning which notes work with each chord shape will take your soloing to the next level, and it will also help you play the melodies of songs.

By trial and error, you can figure out which notes are likely to be useful with any given chord. For example, play a first-position C chord and listen to the harmonious notes (circles in the grid on the left) and notes that sound discordant (circles in the grid on the right).

Harmonious Notes (open circles)   Discordant Notes (open circles)

Using the trial-and-error method of finding useful notes also makes for good ear training. For now, here are some "good notes" that go with first-position D, A, G, and F chords. Practice playing them, and then try the enhanced version of "Rock Ballad" below.

 **4. Rock Ballad #2**

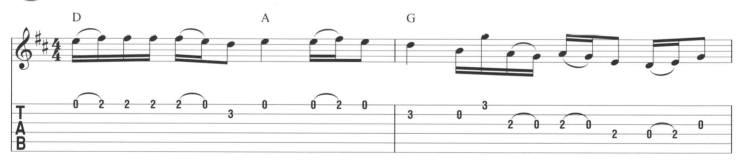

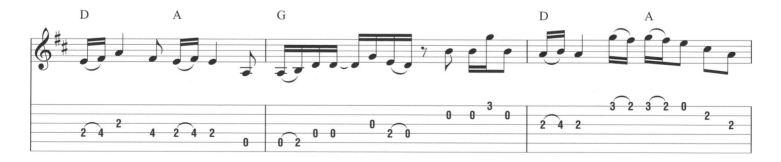

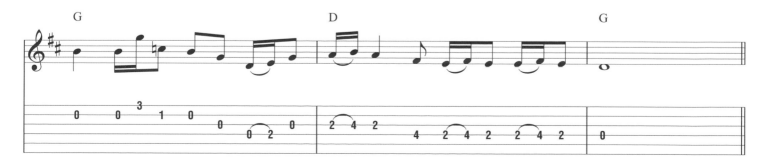

Those "extra notes" that complement the notes of each chord are called *scale tones*, or notes from the major scale. If you play them from lowest to highest in pitch, you have major scales. This example shows the C major scale.

 5. C Major Scale

Play this scale repeatedly, as written, and soon your fingers will know it by heart. Then, try playing familiar tunes in the key of C, such as "This Land Is Your Land" or "Twinkle, Twinkle, Little Star" (hey, it's Mozart!). Remember to play each chord and build the melody from notes within and around the chords.

Here's the melody to "When the Saints Go Marching In," in the key of C, twice around the 16-bar tune. The first time is the bare melody; the second time, the melody is ornamented with hammer-ons, pull-offs, slides, and "extra notes." Notice how little phrases fill the pauses in the song's melody.

Remember, as you play the solos, make the chord changes. Sometimes, when the song goes to the IV (F) or V (G) chord, the melody is found in the major scale of that chord. Other times, it's in the major scale of the I (C) chord.

 6. "When the Saints Go Marching In"

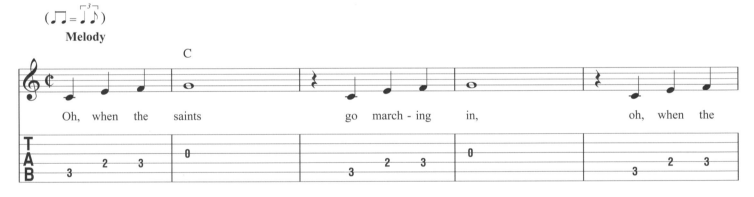

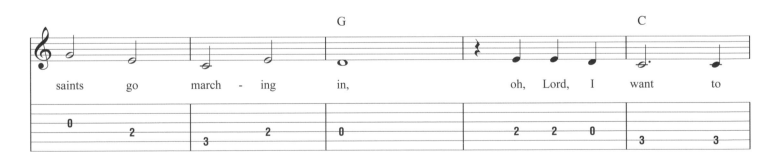

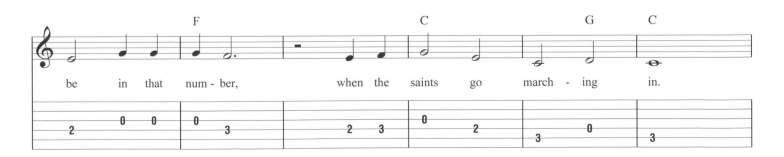

Ornamented Melody

BLUE NOTES

The flatted 3rd, 7th, and 5th tones of the major scale are called "blue notes," because they make a melody sound bluesy! Sprinkle them into your melodies and embellishments, and your solos will sound more interesting. Even if a song is not bluesy, you can play blue notes and immediately resolve them (moving them up or down a fret) to a scale tone.

Here are the blue notes surrounding the I (C), IV (F), and V (G) chords in the key of C:

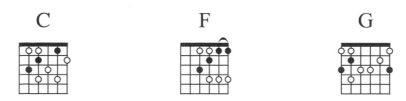

These are used in the following solo to the Bahamian folk song, "Sloop John B." The first solo is the bare melody, and the melody in the second solo is ornamented with blue notes, as well as slides, hammer-ons, and pull-offs.

 7. **"Sloop John B."**

Melody

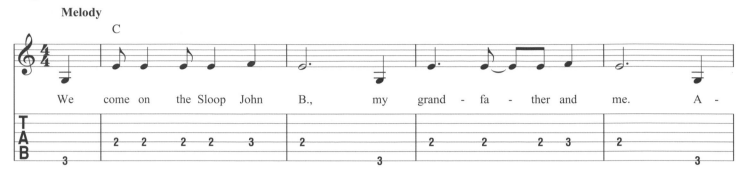

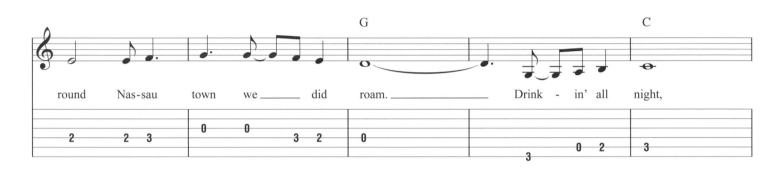

Ornamented Melody

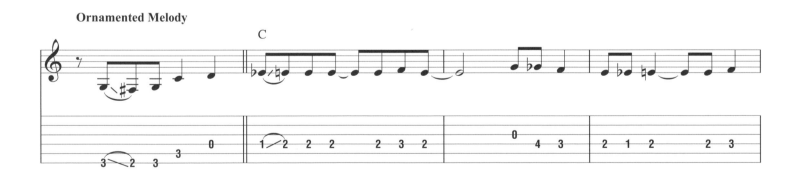

To play solos in the four other easy, first-position guitar keys—G, D, A, and E—go through the steps you took in the key of C.

- Learn the useful scale tones of the I, IV, and V chords (G, C, and D), or if you prefer, learn the major scales for those chords.

- Try to play familiar, easy melodies in each key, making the chord changes and finding melody notes within and around each chord.

- Learn the blue notes for the I, IV, and V chords in G, and then use them (sparingly) in your solos.

OTHER FIRST-POSITION MAJOR SCALES AND BLUE NOTES

At this point, you may have noticed that the harmonious notes that surround each chord are the major scale notes and the blue notes. For example, when you're playing a first-position C chord, the most useful notes for soloing are the notes of the chord itself (C, E, G), plus nearby C major-scale notes (D, F, A, B) and the blue notes (E♭, G♭, B♭) of the C scale. Once you learn the following five first-position major scales and the blue notes of each scale, you'll be able to solo in six keys. (You've already learned the C major scale and blue notes.) Practice each major scale repeatedly, going up and down as written and as heard in the audio file.

 8. G Major Scale

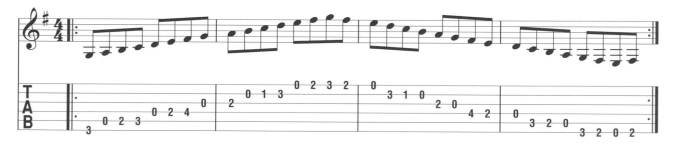

Blue Notes

G

9. D Major Scale

Blue Notes

D

 10. A Major Scale

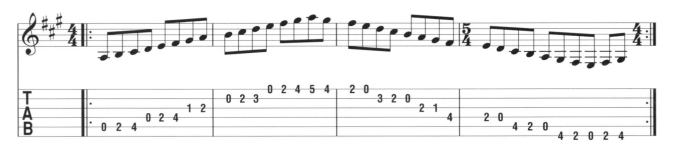

Blue Notes

A

11. E Major Scale

Blue Notes

E

12. F Major Scale

Blue Notes

F

ORNAMENTING A MELODY

The solo for "When the Saints Go Marching In" (Example 6) features a melody that is ornamented with various devices. Here are some of the many ways to vary and embellish a melody.

- Slide up to a melody note from one or two frets back, especially a note that is stressed in the melody (often, this is the note that ends a phrase).

- Hammer-on to a melody note from an open string or from one or two frets back. This is also effective on a stressed note.

- Pull-off to a melody note from a note that is one or two frets higher.

- Play a blue note that is a fret above or below a melody note, then quickly play the actual melody note, by picking, sliding into, or hammering-on to it.

- Dance around a melody note by sandwiching it between adjacent notes.

- Make up brief melodic phrases, using the major scale to fill gaps or pauses in the melody.

Each of these ideas is implemented in the following solo to "Will the Circle Be Unbroken."

The solo appears on the next page to allow for easier reading.

13. "Will the Circle Be Unbroken"

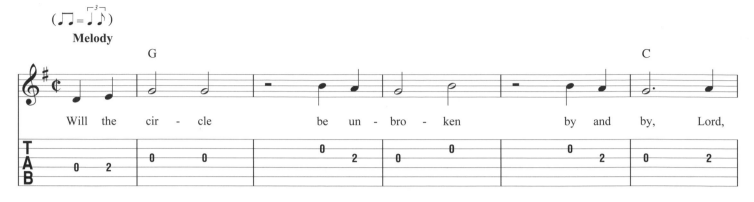

Ornamented Melody

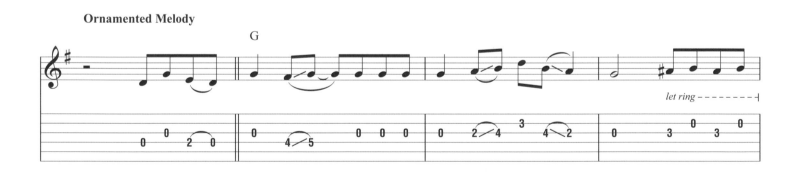

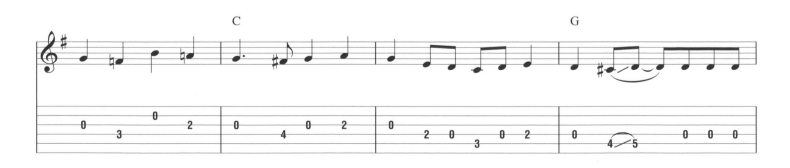

16

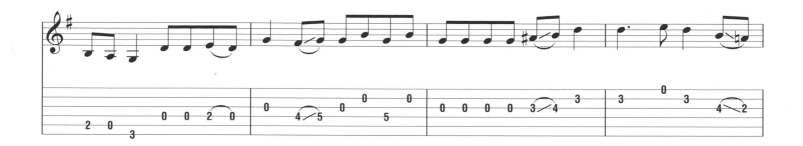

FOLLOWING THROUGH

Here are some tips on how to become adept at chord-based soloing. Follow these instructions, and you will be automatically sprung from scale-jail—well, at least you'll be out on bail!

- Practice one of the major scales (start with the C major scale), looping it and playing it up and down. Repeat it with a steady tempo until it becomes easy to play it quickly and smoothly.

- Pick out simple melodies using this scale.

- Ad-lib solos to simple, three-chord songs in the key of C. Stick as close as you can to the melody, but ornament it as described previously.

- Learn the blue notes in the key of C.

- Ad-lib solos that make use of the blue notes.

- Repeat the same process in the other open-position keys: G, D, A, E, and F. This may mean working on one key for a day, a week, a month, or as long as it takes to become comfortable with that key.

It's good practice to play along with recordings by your favorite artists, as long as you choose fairly simple tunes. Playing along with an excellent band helps you play in time. There's no stopping and starting over, or even slowing down, for the harder parts!

To do this, you need to know the key and the chord changes in advance. You can find guitar chords and lyrics sheets for many songs at *GuitarInstructor.com* or *SheetMusicDirect.com*.

JAILBREAK 3
First-Position/Key-of-E Licks

Here's another non-scale-based soloing strategy. As you'll discover in future chapters, these open-position E licks will not only give you a valuable soloing approach but also lead to greater understanding of up-the-neck electric blues and rock guitar playing. Why? Because those styles grew out of these formative E blues licks.

The key of E has long been a favorite for blues guitarists, including Lightnin' Hopkins, Jimmy Reed, Muddy Waters, Gatemouth Brown, and Arthur Crudup, to name just a few. And if the key of E didn't suit their vocal range, they'd apply a capo up a few frets so they could still play those E licks.

Open-position E isn't just for blues, though; it's a favorite key for rock guitarists as well. Think of songs such as "Susie-Q," "Oh, Pretty Woman," "Day Tripper," "Voodoo Chile," "Are You Gonna Go My Way," "Back in Black," and so on. Electric country guitarists also like to solo in E to get an old-fashioned, bluesy, honky-tonk effect. So here are some E licks to examine:

 14A. Bluesy E Licks

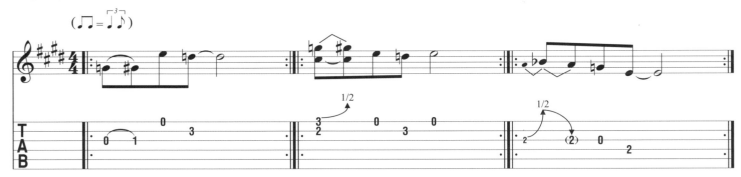

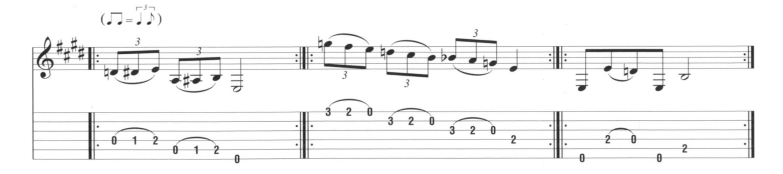

18

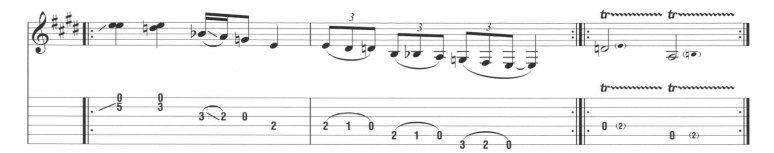

Players who favor the open-position E sometimes play up the neck on the high strings while picking the open low E string with their thumb.

 14B.

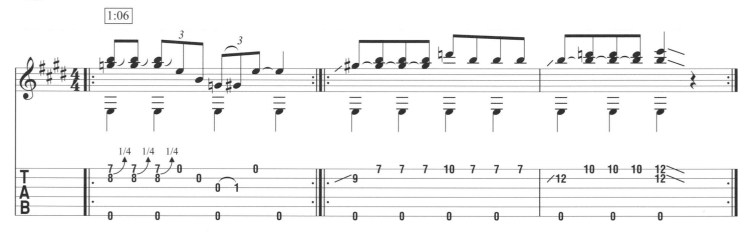

BOOGIE RIFFS

The open-position E chord is a great launching pad for boogie-woogie riffs, which are often used in backup and solos. There are countless variations; here are a few choice riffs using chord tones, scale tones, and blue notes. Note that all of these riffs can also be moved up a string and thus played in the key of A, as you'll see in the final two bars.

 15. Boogie Riffs

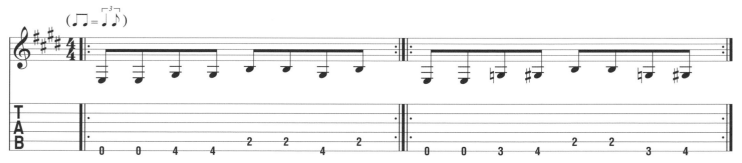

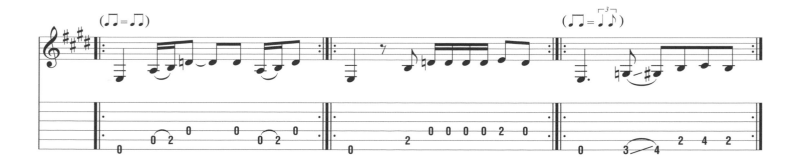

19

SOLOS

The following solos show how to use key-of-E licks in blues, rock, and country contexts.

 16. Blues Solo

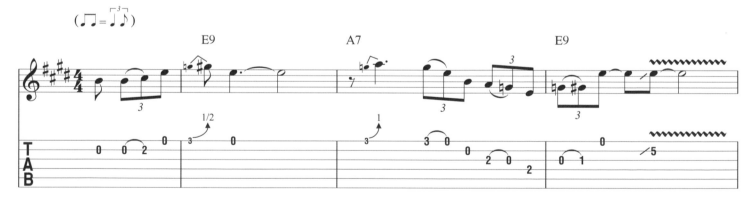

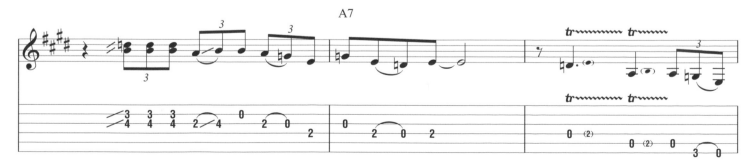

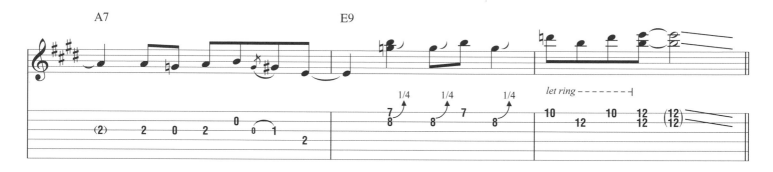

17. Rock Solo

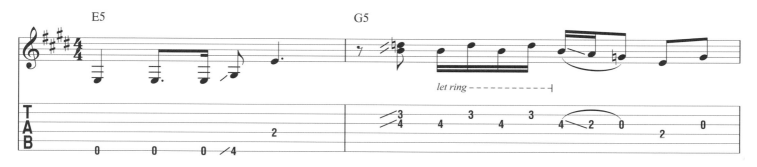

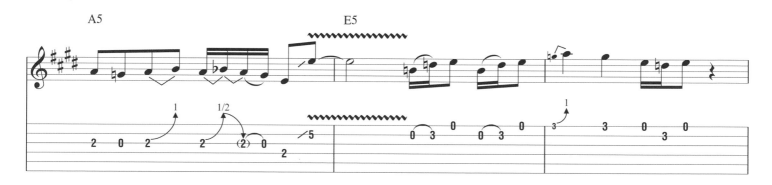

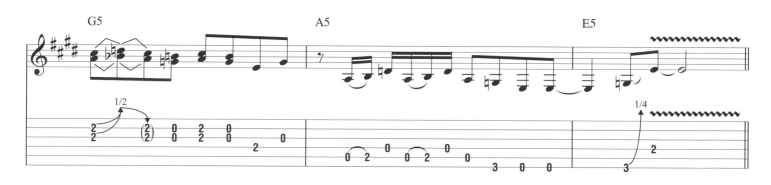

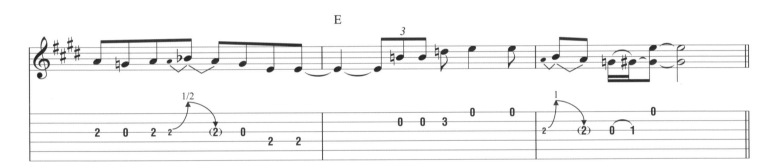

LISTENING SUGGESTIONS

In addition to the songs mentioned earlier in this chapter, check out the following for more examples of playing open-position E riffs and licks.

- "Rollin' Stone" by Muddy Waters

- "Baby Please Don't Go" and "Coffee Blues" by Lightnin' Hopkins

- "Frosty," "Okie Dokie Stomp," and "Born in Louisiana" by Gatemouth Brown

- "That'll Be the Day" by Buddy Holly

JAILBREAK 4
F-Position and Steve Cropper Double-Stop Licks

By now, those scale-jail prison bars should have begun fading from your memory. Let's keep working toward your jailbreak!

In this chapter, you'll explore another chord-based lead guitar style, this one using two-note combinations called *double stops*. Learning how to use double stops will not only expand your lead guitar repertoire but also get you started playing chord-based riffs and solos all over the fretboard.

Guitarist Steve Cropper (Booker T and the MGs) is one of the most famous players to use the double-stop shapes called *6ths* intervals, so called because the two notes that make up the double stop are six scale tones apart. You can hear this double stop in the songs that Cropper recorded for Stax artists like Sam & Dave, Otis Redding, Wilson Pickett, and Carla Thomas, to name just a few. As a result, we're going to call these "Steve Cropper licks."

A BLUES TURNAROUND IN E

This Cropper lick derives from an open-position E blues turnaround, which is a musical phrase that ends many blues verses.

 19A. Steve Cropper Licks

Since the turnaround is played on the first and third strings simultaneously, you need to use your thumb and index finger to play it, or employ *hybrid picking*, using a flatpick and your middle finger.

MAKING IT MOVABLE

A full F chord is the same as a first-position E chord that is barred up a fret. And the F formation (pictured below) is just an abbreviated version of the barred F chord. So you can use that all-important F formation to play the above E blues turnaround (Example 19A) in any key.

The F formation is movable (it has no open strings), and its root is on the first string. In the following example, you fret the F formation at the third fret to play the turnaround lick in G (because the first string/third fret is a G note); then, you fret the F formation at the eighth fret, where the first string is a C note, to play the turnaround in the key of C. In both keys, the turnaround lick ends on the F formation.

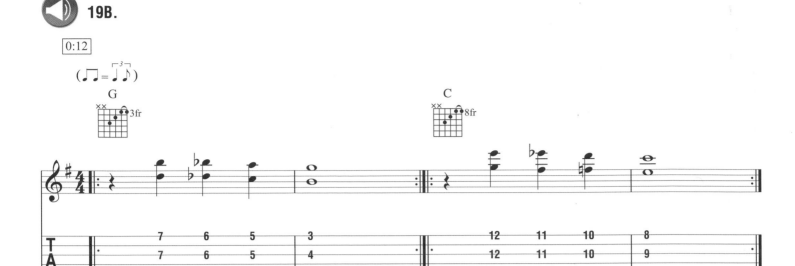

19B.

`0:12`

You can spin countless variations of this lick by starting at the root and ascending (measure 1, below), skipping a middle pair of notes (measure 2), or playing the first and third strings separately (measure 3).

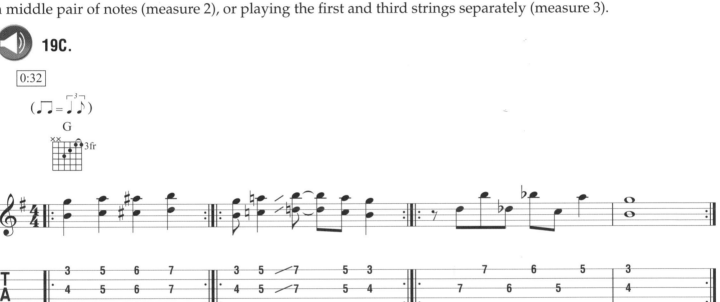

19C.

`0:32`

FOLLOWING THE CHANGES

One of the most effective ways to use the Cropper licks throughout a song is to simply follow the chord changes, using F forms for each chord.

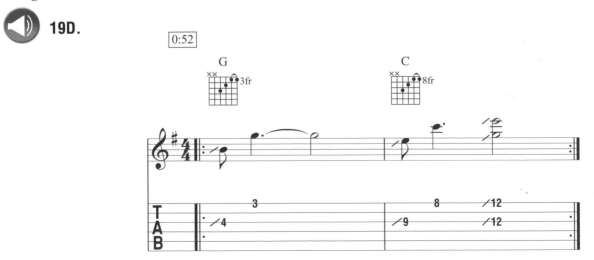

19D.

`0:52`

FILLS FOR ACCOMPANIMENT

Lead guitarists often play variations of the Cropper licks as fills between a vocalist's phrases, as shown in this version of the classic folk/blues song, "Frankie and Johnny." Since the song is a blues in E, you can play variations of the open-position E turnaround. Then, play licks based on the F form at the fifth fret over the change to A and the seventh fret for the B7 chord.

 20. "Frankie and Johnny"

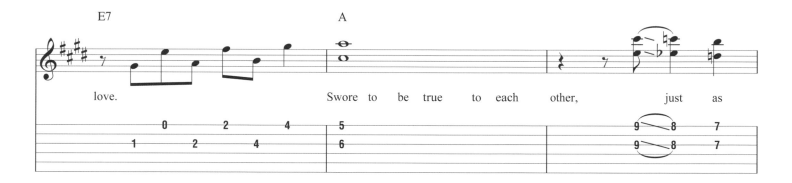

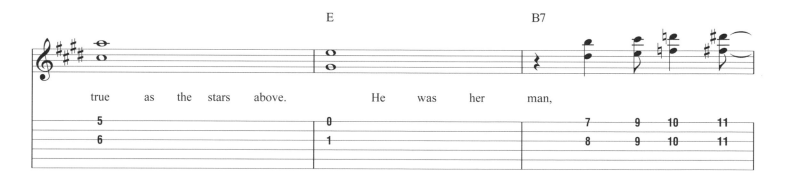

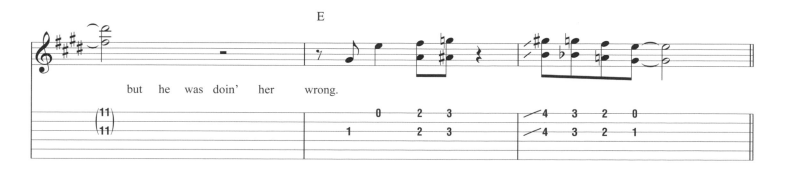

SEVENTH AND NINTH CHORDS

You can play a 7th or 9th chord—which is just a 7th chord with an extra note added for a jazzier sound—by lowering the F formation two frets, or by raising the upper end of the Cropper lick by three frets, still playing just the first and third strings.

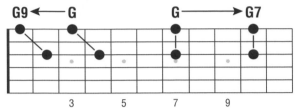

In the following R&B version of the old blues song "Stagolee," the guitar accompaniment includes 7th and 9th chords. The licks are based on F forms at the fifth fret (A chords), tenth fret (D chords), and 12th fret (E chords).

 21. "Stagolee" (Accompaniment)

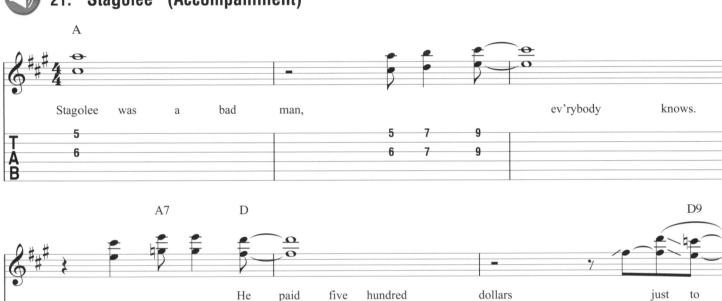

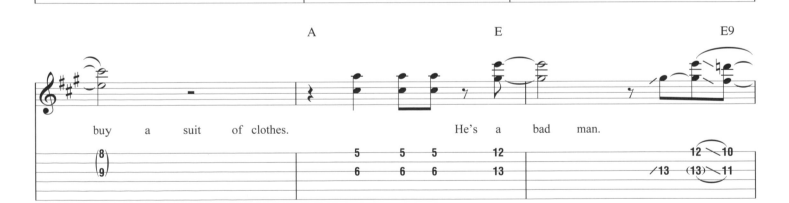

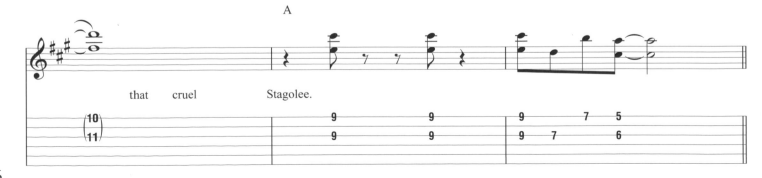

26

Cropper licks can also have that "island" effect, as demonstrated here in "Sloop John B.":

 22. "Sloop John B." (Accompaniment)

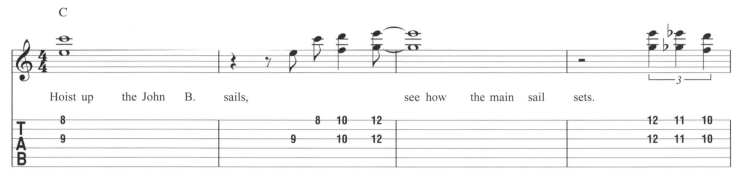

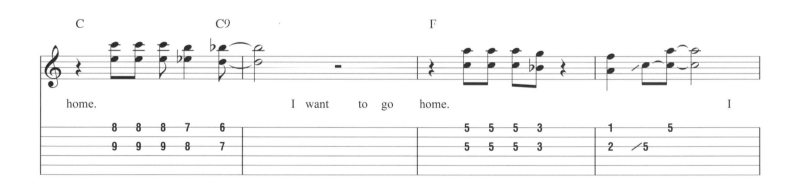

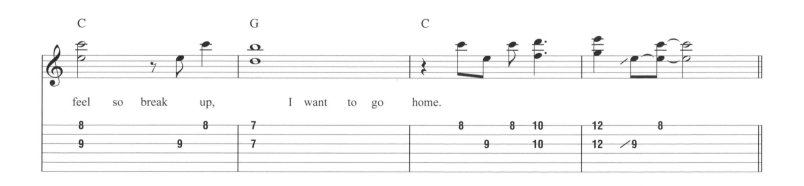

STEVE CROPPER LICKS FOR SOLOING

In addition to accompaniment uses, Cropper licks lend themselves quite well to soloing. In the following solo to "Stagolee," all of the melody is expressed with these double-stop licks, except for the three bars of D (measures 5–7), during which the melody is found in or around the F form of the D chord at the tenth fret.

 23. "Stagolee" (Solo)

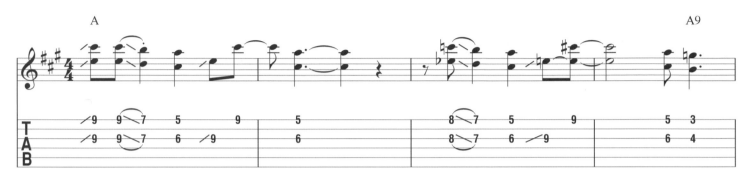

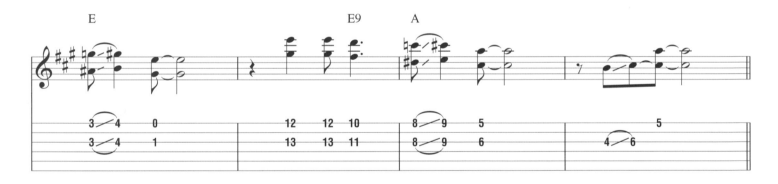

In this solo to the old blues tune, "Stealin'," the two-note Cropper licks carry most of the melody.

 24. "Stealin'" (Accompaniment and Solo)

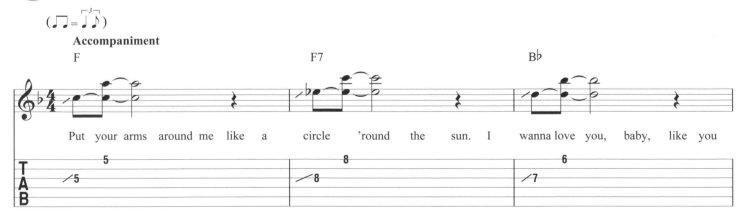

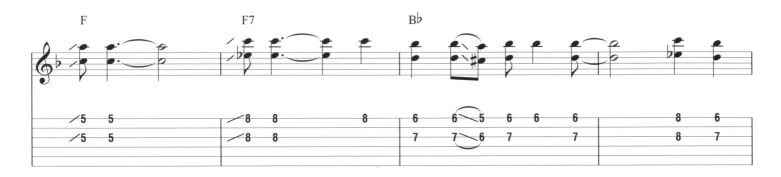

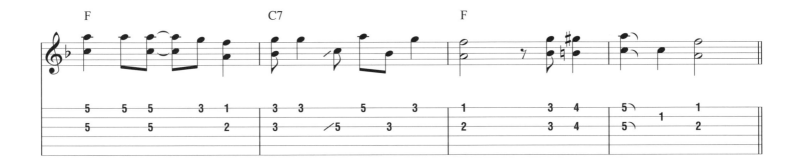

LISTENING AND PRACTICING SUGGESTIONS

- "Hold On, I'm Comin'" by Sam and Dave

- "She Belongs to Me" and "Love Minus Zero/No Limit" by Bob Dylan

- Play along with simple, three-chord tunes (jam tracks or popular songs) and practice your Steve Cropper licks.

JAILBREAK 5
F-Position and Chuck Berry Double-Note Licks

Here's a powerful shovel to help you keep digging your way out of scale-jail: The F position and the licks based on it have generated countless classic rock, blues, and country solos!

Besides being a great songwriter and performer, Chuck Berry was one of the first rock guitar heroes. He created *the* early rock guitar soloing style that has been imitated by countless guitarists for decades and to this day. Though he modestly claimed he was just imitating his musical idols, such as T-Bone Walker and Carl Hogan (guitarist for Louis Jordan and His Tympany Five), Berry's double-stop licks presented a new twist on electric blues guitar, and they were instantly recognizable as an exciting and dynamic sound.

Much of Chuck Berry's soloing was based on that movable F form that drives so many guitar licks and styles. Remember: Because the F shape is movable, the following licks can be played in any key.

 25. Chuck Berry Licks

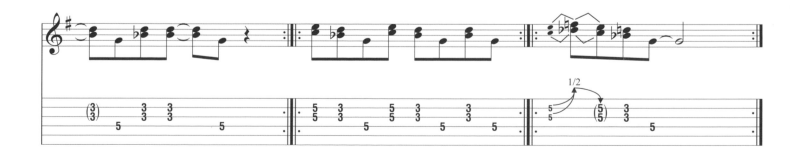

31

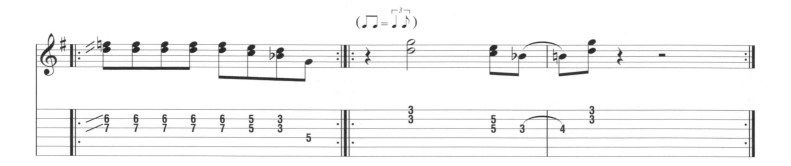

If you're playing these licks correctly, your left hand should keep coming back to the F shape. Play them over a 12-bar blues, and you'll find that most of them work over all three chords (I, IV, V).

FILLS

You can use these licks as fills, or "response" phrases that fill the pauses in a vocal line. Sometimes, as in the sample below, the fills mimic the vocal melody. Since the song is in the key of A, play the F formation at the fifth fret, and use the licks you played in Example 25, only two frets higher.

 26. "Fourteen Years"

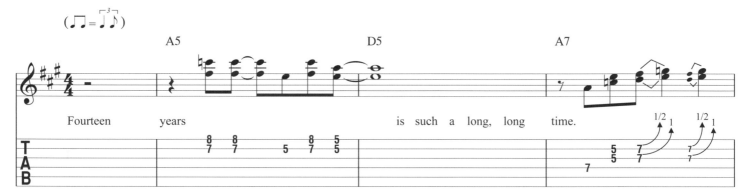

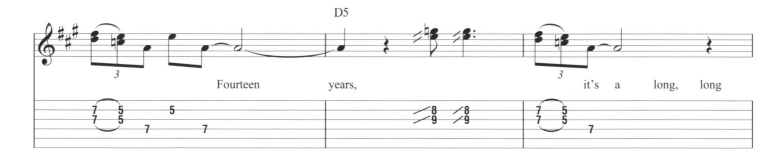

you just don't stop on a dime.

AD-LIBBING SOLOS

You can also use double-stop licks to build solos. Here's a sample solo in G, with a straight-eighths rock beat:

 27. Double-Stop Rock in G

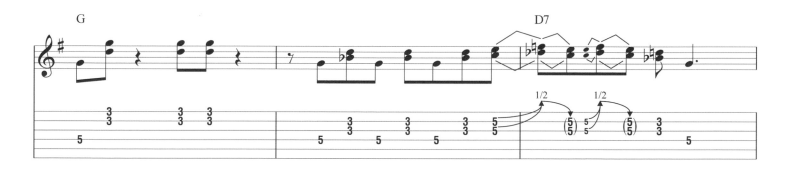

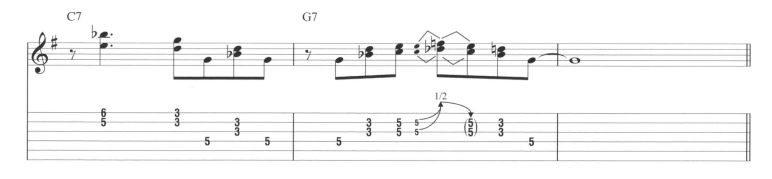

Move the same licks up to the fifth fret to play this shuffle-beat blues in the key of A.

 28. Shuffle-Beat Blues in A

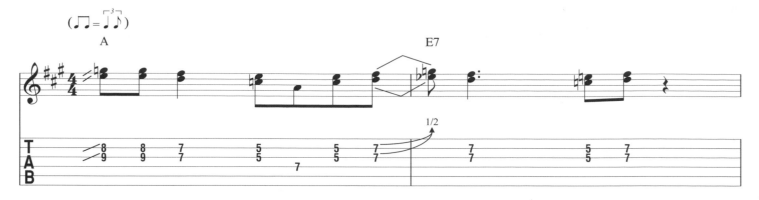

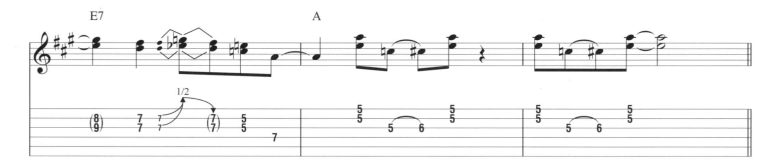

PLAYING A MELODY

Sometimes your Chuck Berry-style solo can simulate a melody, as in "See See Rider," below. It's in the key of C, so the F form-based licks are moved up to the eighth fret. The first time around this old 12-bar folk-blues tune, the guitar plays "response" licks between vocal phrases—a very common blues practice. The second time around, the solo approximates the song's melody.

 29. "See See Rider" (Response Licks)

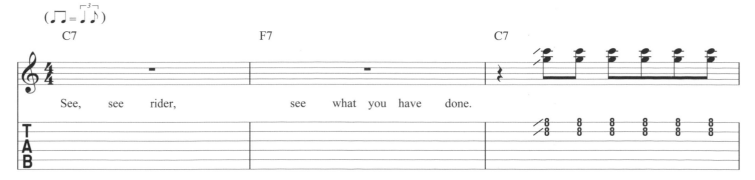

34

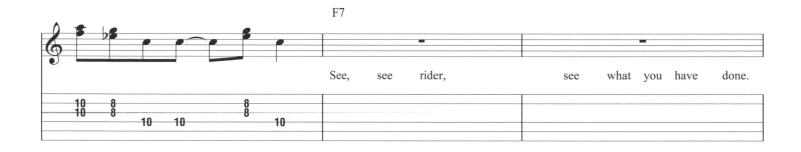

See, see rider, see what you have done.

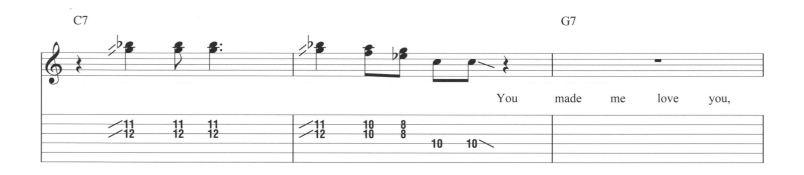

You made me love you,

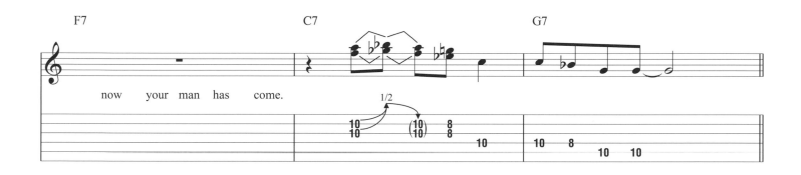

now your man has come.

Solo

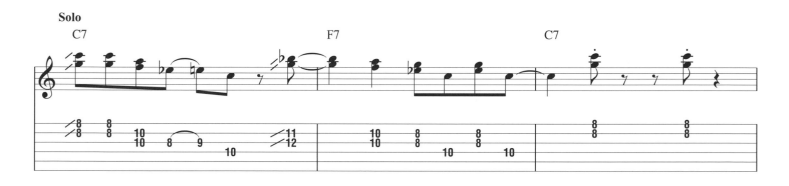

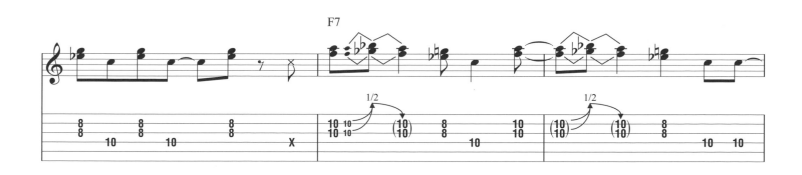

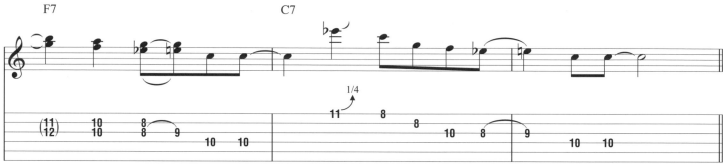

FOLLOWING THROUGH

Besides imitating Berry's style, as in the above solos, you can spice up your single-note electric blues, country, or rock solos with occasional Chuck Berry-style double-stop licks. They fatten up your solos, as you'll see in the next chapter on minor pentatonic scales. They also help make scale-jail a distant memory.

JAILBREAK 6
Movable Minor Pentatonic Scales

OK, you're back to scales. But these scales won't imprison you, if you know how to use them.

In the first chapter, you learned some foundational blues licks. The movable minor pentatonic scale, or "blues box," grew out of those licks, and it's the basis for modern electric blues as well as much rock guitar soloing.

The blues box is so named because it has a box-like shape on the fretboard. In proper music terminology, it's called a *minor pentatonic scale*:

- *Minor* because it includes the flatted 3rd.

- *Pentatonic* because it consists of five tones: 1–♭3–4–5–♭7.

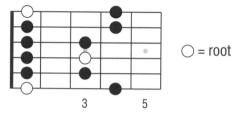

As mentioned before, the "blues box" is the primary, go-to soloing device for most blues and rock guitarists, and it's often useful in modern country and jazz as well. It's the first soloing strategy most would-be lead guitarists learn because it enables you to play credible solos to countless blues and rock tunes, even if you have no clue what you're doing! If you stick to the notes in the scale, it's difficult to make a mistake, to which most guitar students enthusiastically say, "Sign me up for that!"

The downside, however, is that your solos won't sound like much unless you:

A. Learn the characteristic blues-rock licks that allow you to "speak the language of the blues."

B. Become so familiar with the various blues scale positions that you can hear the notes and licks in your mind, before you play them. Only then can you play intentionally as opposed to blindly running up and down the scales.

The first part—learning the licks—is simple. Just as you learned your native language by imitating how adults speak, you can develop a blues vocabulary by imitating the licks of your favorite electric blues guitarists. There are countless music/tablature books and websites that have transcriptions of solos by famous blues guitarists, and learning some excellent solos by rote will help you learn essential, generic blues licks.

The second part—learning where the notes are—is trickier because it means developing your ear, rather than just memorizing solos. Learning to play familiar melodies with the blues boxes can help in this process. That's why many of the solos that follow express the melody of a well-known song or embellish the melody and ad-lib around it, without losing it entirely.

MAKING THE E-BLUES LICKS MOVABLE

T-Bone Walker is often credited as the father of modern electric blues guitar. In the 1940s, he figured out how to make those open-position E-blues licks movable, so that he could play them in any key, all over the fretboard of his electric guitar.

The key to making the E licks movable is recognizing that a movable F chord is just an E chord with a barre behind it. The shapes are shown on the next page.

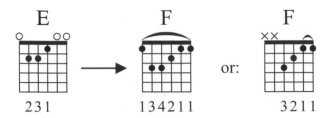

Once you understand this simple fact, you can play any E lick in the key of F. Every note is one fret higher than it was in E, and open strings are now fretted at the first fret.

 30. Movable E-Blues Licks

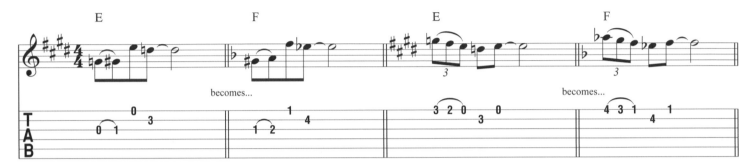

The "F version" of the E licks is movable because it makes use of no open strings, so you can play the E licks in any key. The first string is the root of the F shape, so use that string to position your fretting hand. For example, to play in the key of A, fret the F shape at the fifth fret because the note there on the first string is an A.

MOVABLE BLUES LICKS IN A SOLO

Here are some more movable blues licks based on the F form. They're strung together in a solo to the old blues tune "See See Rider." The melody is stated simply, followed by an improvised solo.

 31. "See See Rider" (Melody and Solo)

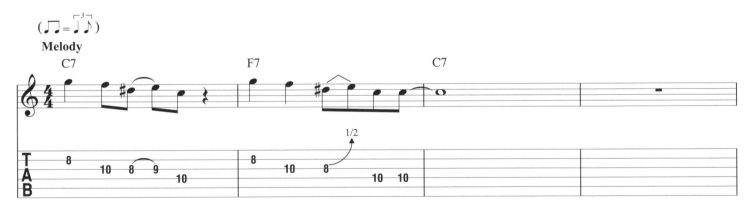

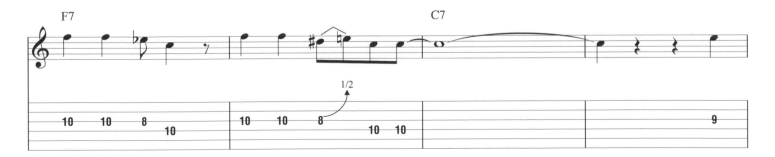

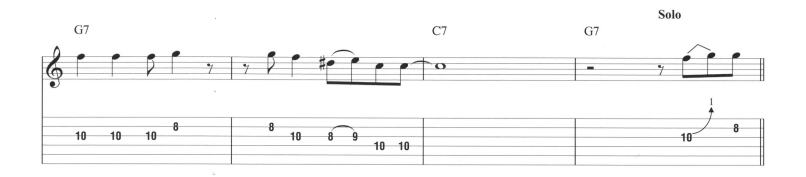

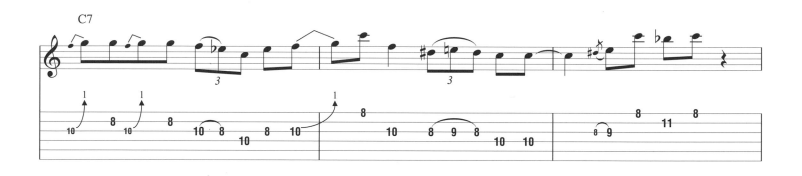

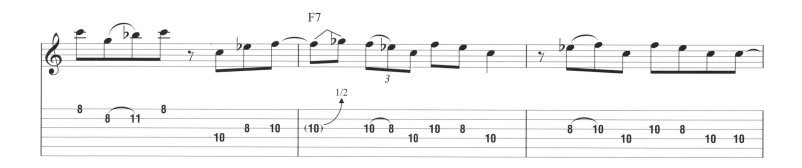

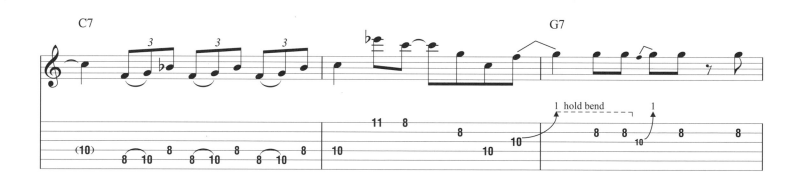

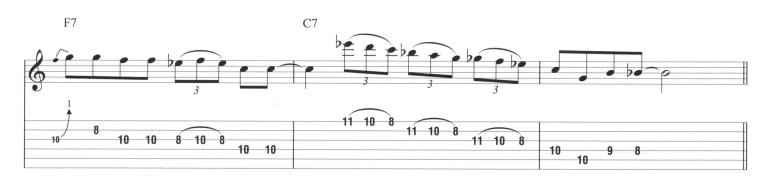

THE BLUES BOX REVISITED

Below you'll see the same minor pentatonic blues box shape you learned earlier in this chapter, but this time, it's in the key of G (F form at the third fret), and it indicates which notes (squares) are commonly used for bending. Again, you can move this shape to any key by finding the root on the first string.

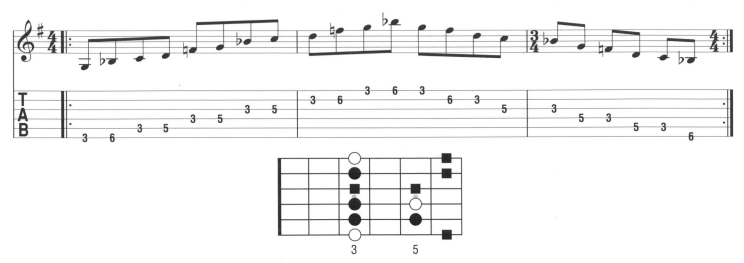

Although that shape will serve you well as it is, it does leave out the "in-between" notes that are often played in blues licks and solos. You can restore some blues subtleties by adding the "in-between" notes indicated by the open circles shown in the blues box diagram here.

G Blues Box With "In-Between Notes"

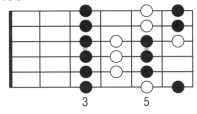

SOLOING IN A MINOR KEY

You can use the first blues box to solo in a minor key. Here are two solos to a rock version of the old folk tune "Rising Sun Blues (The House of the Rising Sun)," in A minor. As before, first play the melody and then play a solo that ornaments it.

 32. "Rising Sun Blues (The House of the Rising Sun)"

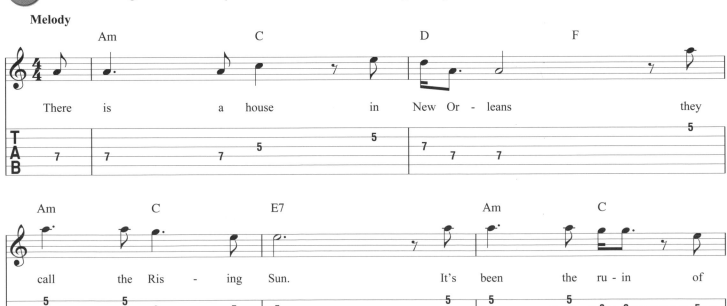

man-y poor girls, ___ and God, I know ___ I'm one.

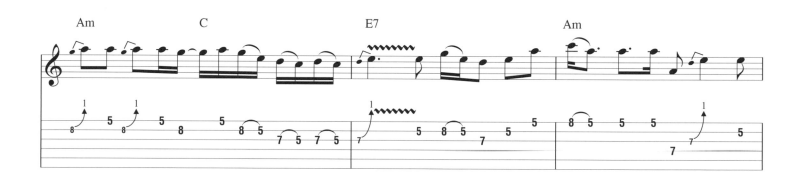

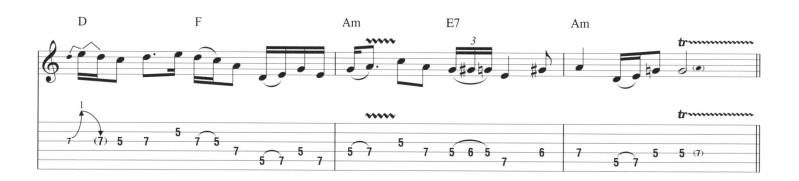

Turn to the next page for more tips on blues-box soloing.

SOLOING IN NON-BLUESY SONGS WITH THE BLUES BOX

If a song's melody is based on the *major* scale with few or no blue notes included, there's a good chance that solos based on the blues box will clash and sound completely inappropriate. But there's still a way to use the blues box shape and its licks in these instances: simply move it down three frets. In other words, if the song is in the key of D, instead of playing the blues box at the tenth fret, play it at the seventh fret.

Wait... Why does "going down three frets" work, you ask? It has to do with a music theory phenomenon called the *relative minor*. See, every major scale has a relative minor scale, which starts on the sixth degree of the major scale. For example, in the D major scale (D–E–F#–G–A–B–C#), the note B is the sixth degree, so B minor is the relative minor scale to D major. Specifically, if you play the notes of the D major scale but start on the B note (B–C#–D–E–F#–G–A), you're playing a B minor scale. But if you look at those two scales, you see that they share the same notes! And on the guitar, the note B is three frets down from the note D.

This same process also works with the blues box shape. If you move the shape from the tenth fret, in D, down three frets to the seventh fret, you get B minor pentatonic, which contains the same five notes as the D major pentatonic. The following solo to "Amazing Grace" offers a great example of this at work.

 33. "Amazing Grace"

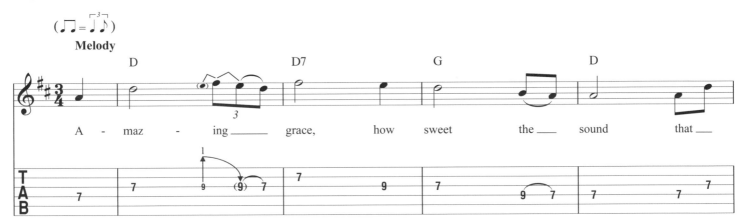

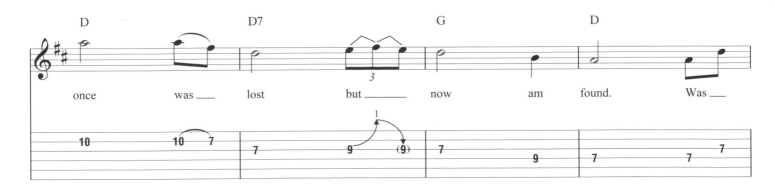

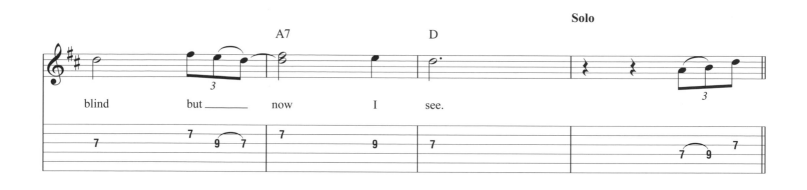

blind   but ___ now   I   see.

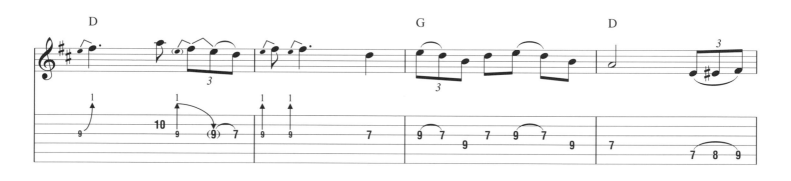

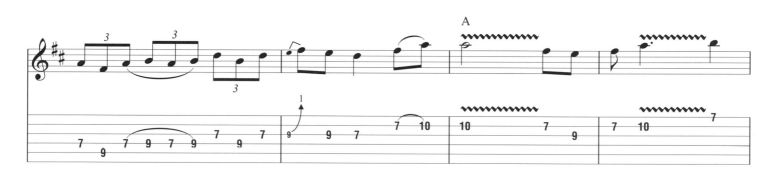

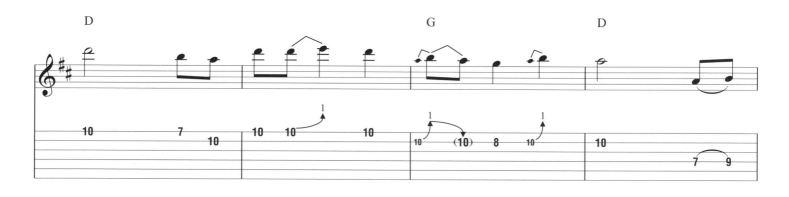

let ring - - - - - - - |

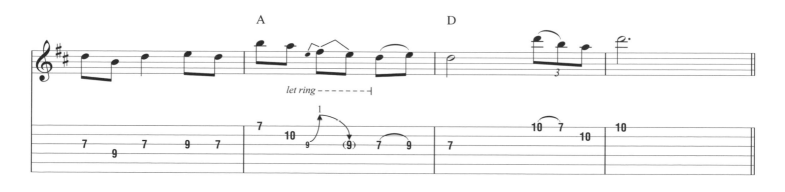

THE SECOND BLUES BOX AND ITS LICKS

There are four blues boxes, or soloing positions, for any given key. Each one is higher up the neck than the last one, which means that in any tune, you can solo in four different registers—up high, down low, or in-between. The multiple positions offer freedom of movement—the opposite of being in scale-jail.

Each blues box relates to a chord position. The second box relates to the open D7 shape, which when played at the sixth fret, is a G7 chord.

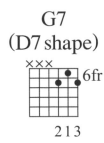

G7
(D7 shape)

Here is the shape of the second blues box as it appears on the fretboard in the key of G:

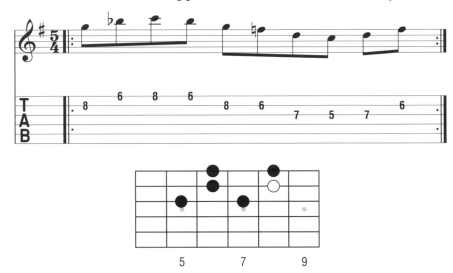

And here it is with bluesy "in-between" notes added (indicated by squares):

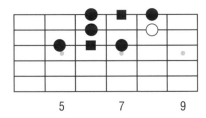

Here are some typical bluesy licks that spring from the second blues box. They're strung together to form a solo over a 12-bar blues in A. They may remind you of Albert King, a very widely imitated blues guitarist who played many of his most characteristic licks in this position.

 34. Blues/Rock in A: Second Blues Box

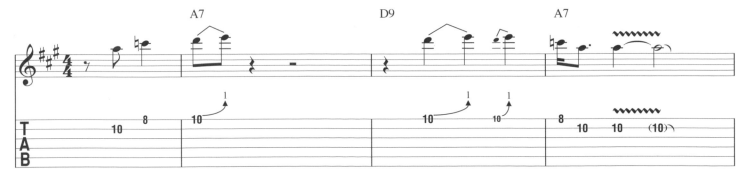

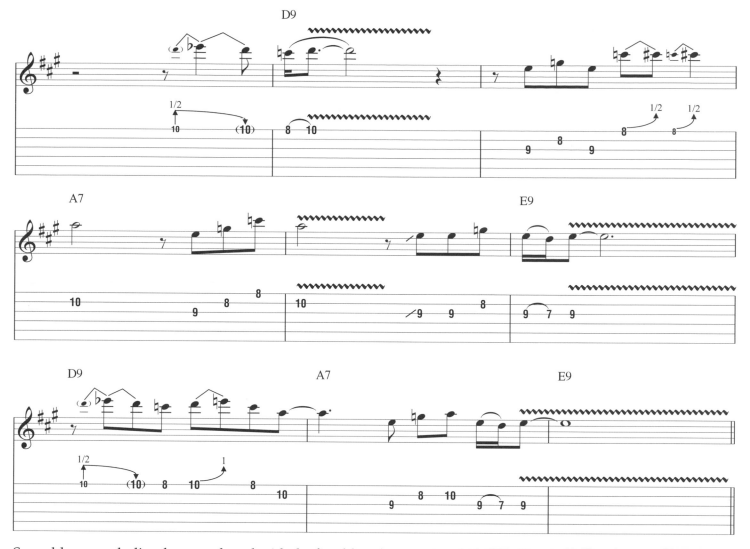

Some bluesy melodies that are played with the first blues box can be played in a higher register, using the second blues box. For example, here's a rendering of "See See Rider" that loses none of the melody despite shifting it from the first blues box (see Example 31) to the second box.

 35. "See See Rider" (Second Blues Box)

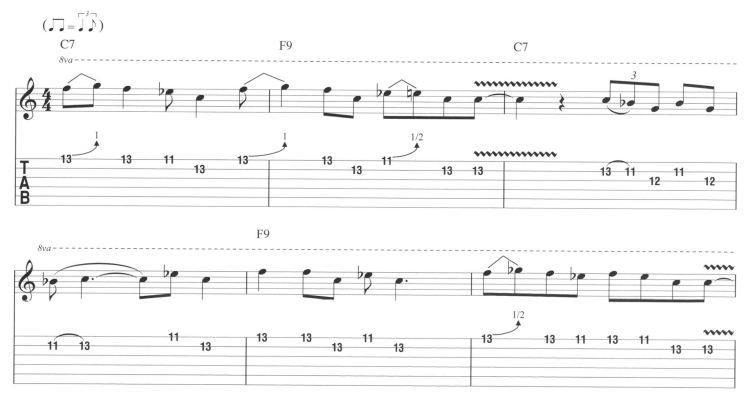

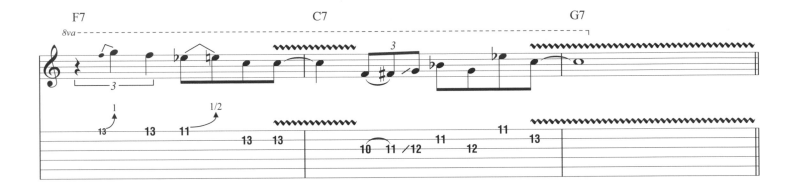

SECOND-BLUES-BOX SOLOING IN A MINOR KEY

Just like the first blues box, the second box works as a soloing strategy in a minor key. In the following gospel tune, "Wayfaring Stranger," the first solo states the melody using the first blues box, whereas the second solo is improvised from the second box.

 36. "Wayfaring Stranger"

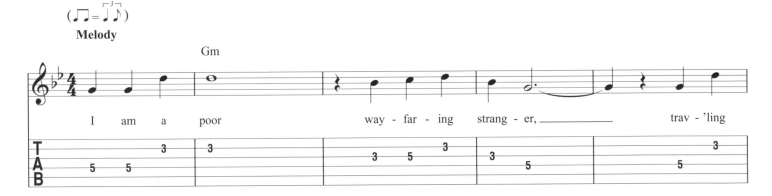

46

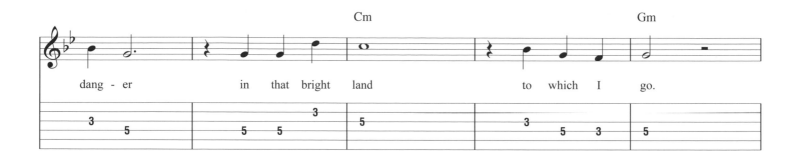

dang - er   in that bright land   to which I go.

Solo

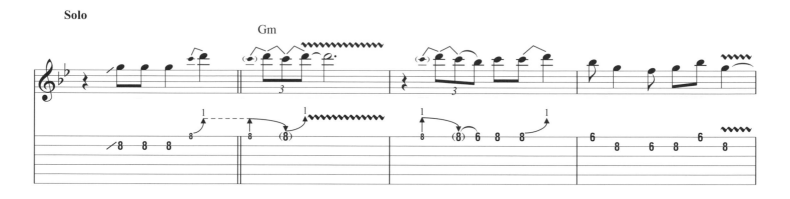

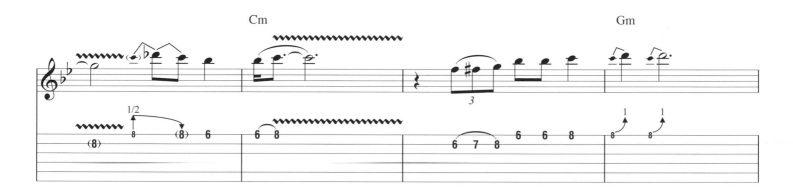

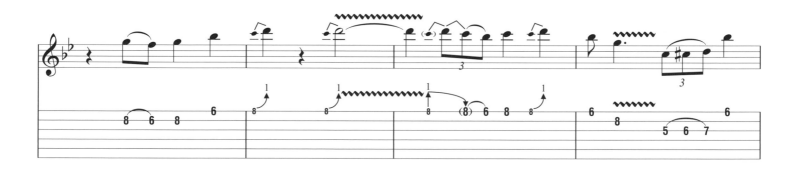

SECOND-BLUES-BOX SOLOING IN NON-BLUESY SONGS

When second-blues-box soloing clashes with a tune, take it down three frets, just as you did with the first blues box. In Example 37, you'll hear the melody of the popular bluegrass tune "Nine Pound Hammer" played twice in the key of A. The first solo makes use of the first blues box at the second fret, three frets lower than the fifth-fret A box. The second solo is based on the second box, also three frets below the usual A position.

 37. "Nine Pound Hammer"

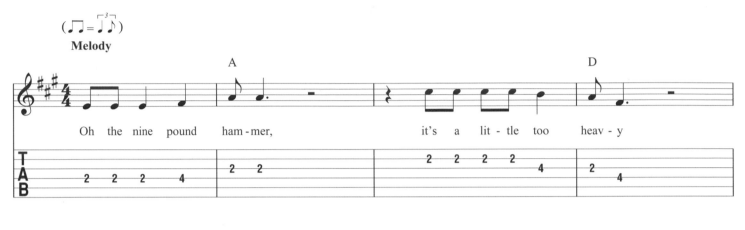

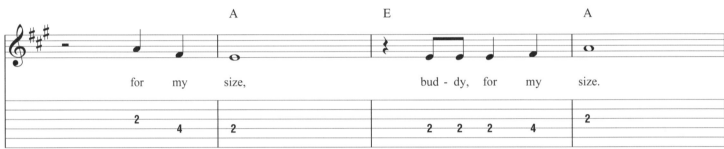

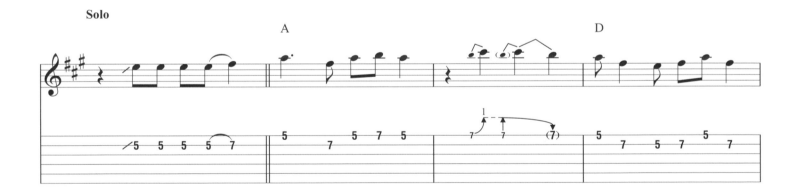

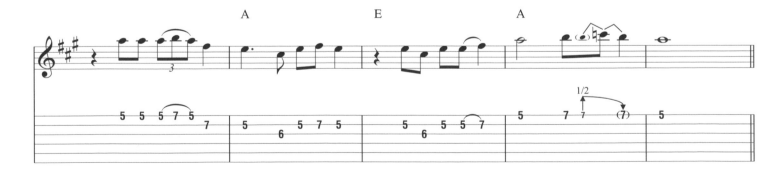

THE THIRD BLUES BOX AND ITS LICKS

You can access the third blues box by playing an F shape a 4th above your key (five frets higher). For example, if a song is in G, play the F shape at the eighth fret, which is a C chord and a 4th above G.

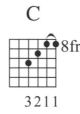

This gets your fretting hand in position to play the third box, shown here:

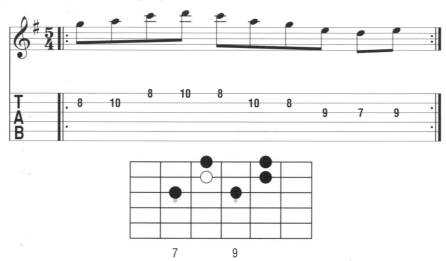

And here it is with the "in-between" notes, for a more bluesy flavor, indicated with squares:

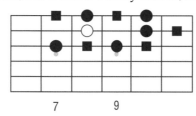

Here are some licks from the third blues box, played over a blues-rock tune in A. They sound more like B.B. King than Albert King, since B.B. played many of his signature licks out of the third blues box.

 38. Blues/Rock in A

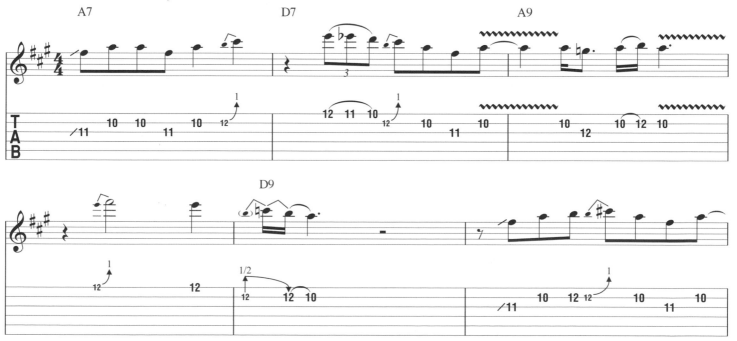

THIRD-BLUES-BOX SOLOING IN NON-BLUESY SONGS

When the third blues box is played correctly (the way B.B. King, Buddy Guy, Otis Rush, Freddie King, and other pioneers of electric blues guitar employed it), it differs from the other three boxes. This is because it contains some major scale notes and lends itself to major-sounding licks, as opposed to strictly minor pentatonic ones.

Although it's useful in typical blues songs, it can also be used as a soloing platform in non-bluesy tunes—and you don't need to lower it three frets below the actual key to do so. In fact, it will clash terribly if you do!

The old Appalachian ballad "Come All You Fair and Tender Ladies" is based on a major scale. It's played below in the key of D in two different ways:

1.   The first solo states the melody simply, employing the seventh-position D major scale.

2.   The second solo ornaments the melody, using the third blues box for the key of D. Normally, you'd locate that box by playing the F shape at the 15th fret, where it's a G chord (the IV chord of D). But in this instance, the F shape is played at the third fret—an octave below the 15th-fret F shape. So it's still an F-shape G chord, and all the licks are the same as if you were playing it at the 15th fret.

 39. "Come All You Fair and Tender Ladies"

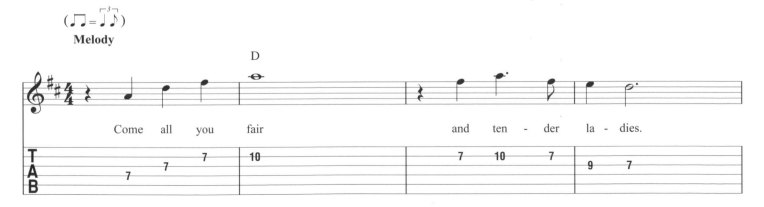

50

Take warn - ing how   you court your men.

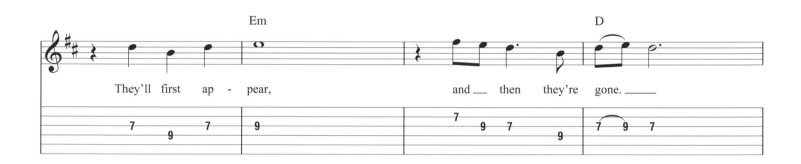

They've like a star   of a sum - mer morn - ing.

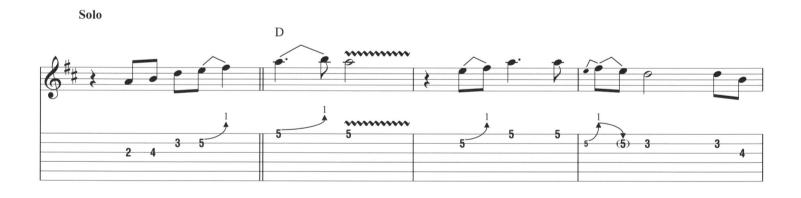

They'll first ap - pear,   and __ then they're gone. _____

Solo

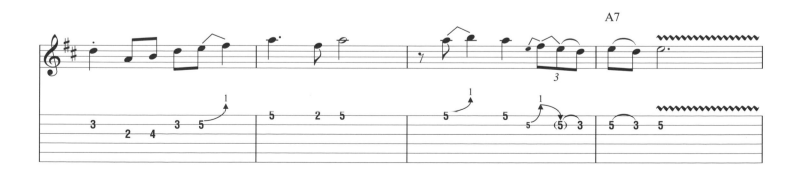

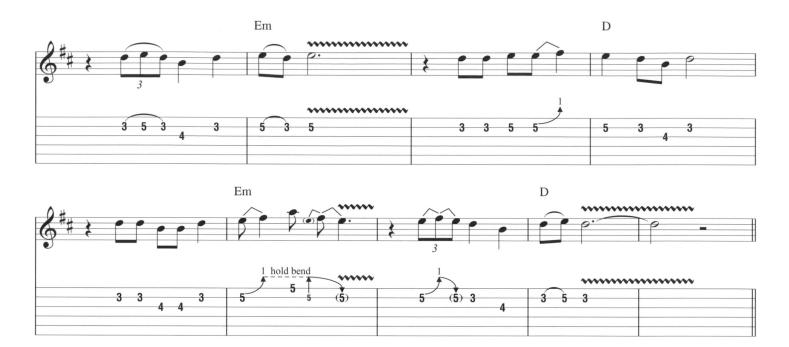

THE FOURTH BLUES BOX AND ITS LICKS

The fourth blues box relates to the following minor chord shape:

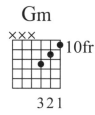

Here's the fourth blues box shape, in G:

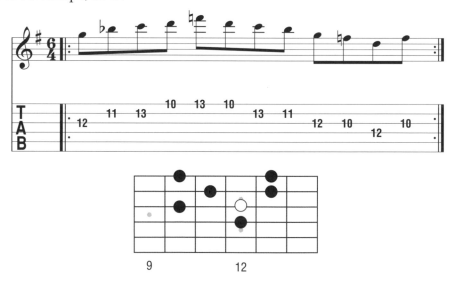

And here it is with the "in-between" notes:

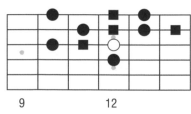

Like the first and second blues boxes, it can be used as a platform for soloing in bluesy songs and songs in a minor key. It can also be used in non-bluesy songs, if you play it three frets below the actual key. The next song, "St. James Infirmary," is an old, minor-key folk-blues song. The first solo states the melody, and the second features some licks typically drawn from the fourth blues box.

40. "St. James Infirmary Blues"

It was down in Old Joe's bar-room, at the cor-ner of ___ the square. ___

The drinks were served as u-sual, and the u-su-al crowd was there.

Solo

AN EASY WAY TO LOCATE THE FOUR BLUES BOXES

The chart below shows a simplified way to locate all four blues boxes, using two-finger, abbreviated versions of the chords to which each box relates. The chart shows the four key-of-G positions, but you can use it to locate the boxes in any key, if you start with the relevant F position for the first box.

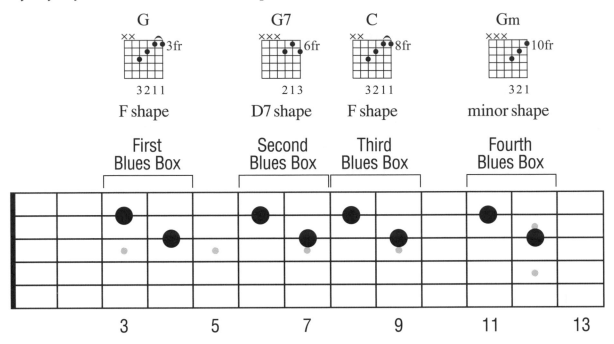

FOLLOWING UP

These three follow-up practices will make the blues scale a liberating force in your quest to get out of scale-jail.

1. Listen to blues and classic rock players like the three Kings (B.B., Freddie, and Albert), Eric Clapton, Buddy Guy, Otis Rush, Jimmy Page, and others to hear and imitate blues phrases, licks, and solos. Practice by jamming along with their recordings.

2. Use the "three frets down" method to jam along with recordings of rock, pop, or country songs that are not bluesy. Find a recorded song's key, and place the blues box three frets lower than that key.

3. Try playing the melody (or a close approximation of it) to blues and bluesy rock songs, using the four blues boxes as soloing platforms. This develops your ear and your familiarity with the notes of each position, and it will help you ultimately play coherent solos.

JAILBREAK 7
Movable Major Scales

Many professional musicians will tell you: "If I can hear it in my mind, I can play it on my axe." And many more aspiring musicians strive to get to that point. Learning major scales is one way to get there. Once you've played a major scale so often that your fingers know where the notes are before you play them, it becomes easier to play whatever melody you have in your head.

Six open-position major scales were presented in the Chapter 1, and you learned solos in three of them—C, G, and D. There are also movable major scales (containing no open strings), and learning them makes it easier to play in any key all over the fretboard.

BASING MOVABLE MAJOR SCALES ON MOVABLE CHORD FORMATIONS

When you're learning movable major scales, it's helpful to associate them with chord forms. Since you've already learned licks based on movable major chord shapes, it should be fairly easy to use those forms to play major scales.

THE F-SHAPE MAJOR SCALE

The F-shape at the third fret is a G chord, and the G major scale written below is based on that chord form. You don't have to play the chord shape constantly while practicing the scale—just hover around that shape and use it as a frame of reference. The first scale is on the top four strings, and the second scale is on the lower strings. Play each shape repeatedly, using the fingering suggestions in the fretboard diagram.

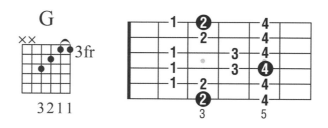

 41. G Major Scale (F Shape)

"Wreck of the Old 97," which tells the story of a train wreck that occurred in 1903, has been recorded by countless country and bluegrass musicians. In the arrangement below, the melody is played in the key of G, using the F shape-based major scale. The second time around, the same major scale is used, but with ornamentation.

 42. "Wreck of the Old 97"

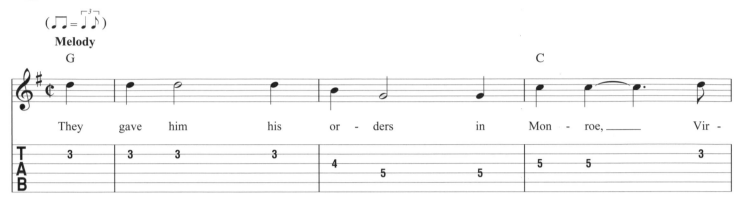

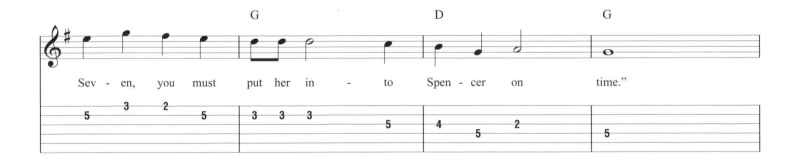

Solo

Because the F-shape major scale is movable, you could play the exact same "Wreck of the Old 97" solo in the key of A, by fretting the F shape at the fifth fret. This way, you can play in practically any key, simply by moving the F shape accordingly.

THE D-SHAPE MAJOR SCALE

Let's take a look at the movable, D-shape major scale pattern:

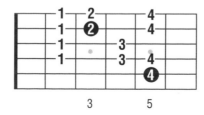

Practice the movable scale on the next page while hovering over the movable D shape.

43. D Major Scale (D Shape)

"Aura Lee" is an old Civil War tune that formed the basis for Elvis Presley's 1956 hit "Love Me Tender." It's shown here in the key of E, so you'll need to move your D-shape scale up two frets. The first time around, the melody is played; the second solo is an improvisation, with some traces of the original melody intact. Note that, despite the many chords in this song, you can still build a solo using the major scale.

44. "Aura Lee"

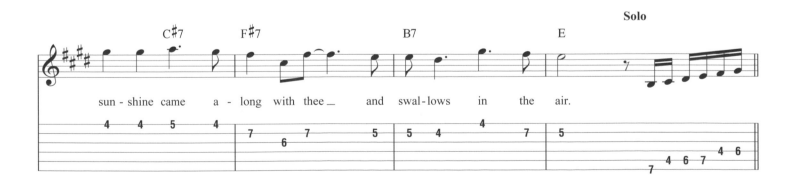

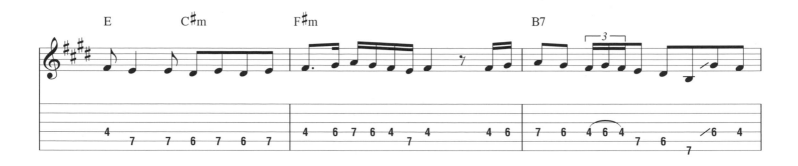

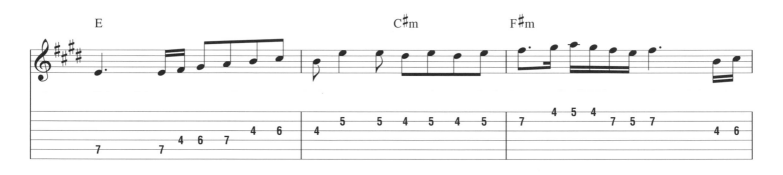

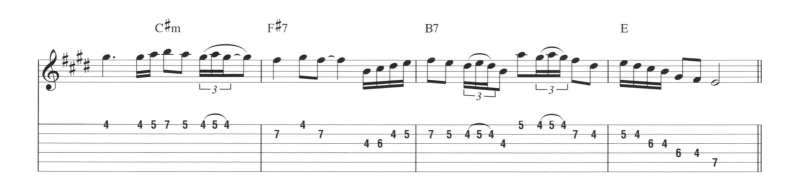

THE A-SHAPE MAJOR SCALE

Here's the movable, A shape-based major scale, played at the fifth fret, which makes it a C major scale.

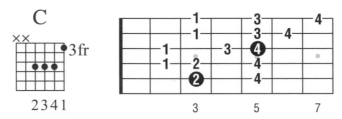

Practice this scale before you play the following solos for the old folk-blues tune "Careless Love." The ad-lib solo has a swing feel.

 45. C Major Scale (A Shape)

 46. "Careless Love"

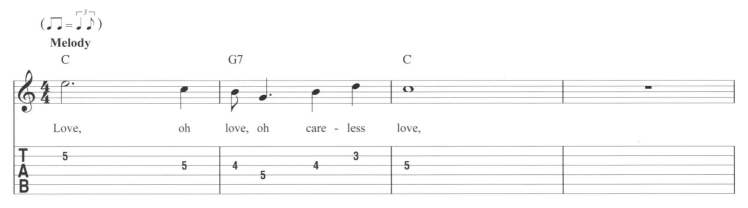

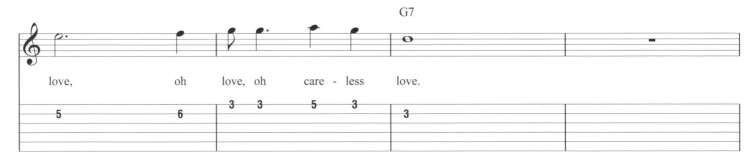

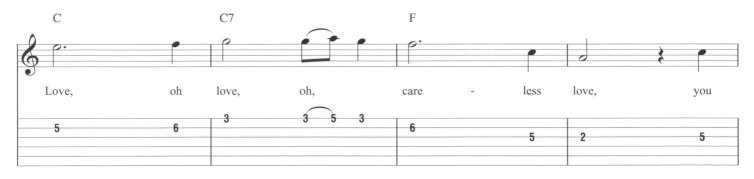

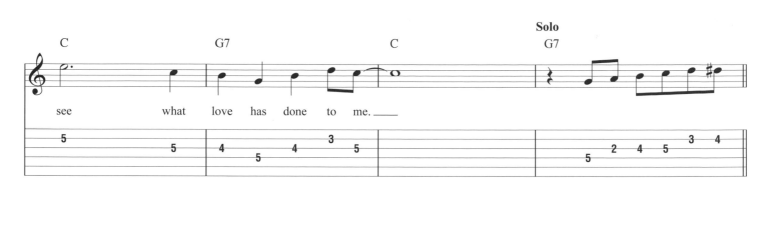

see   what   love   has   done   to   me. ____

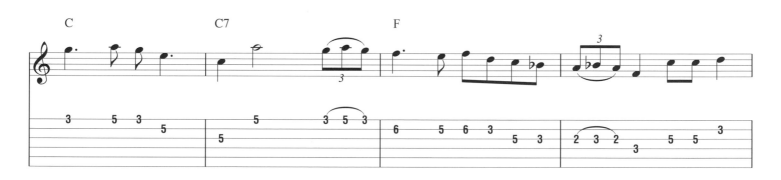

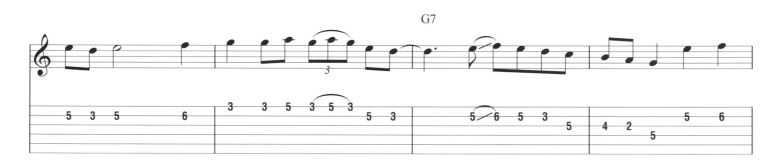

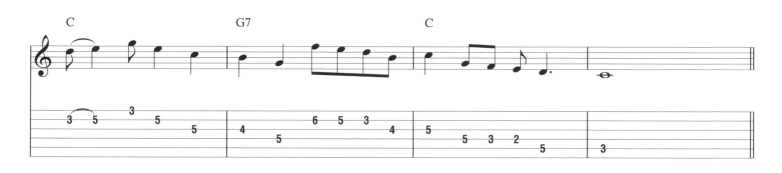

ANOTHER A-SHAPE MAJOR SCALE

Here's an alternative major scale pattern based on the A shape.

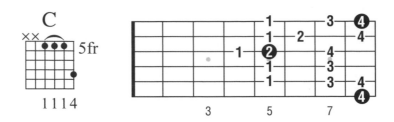

Practice the major scale that goes with this A-shape form, and then play the rock-style solo to the mid-1800s song "Oh, Shenandoah."

 47. C Major Scale (Alternate Shape)

 48. "Oh, Shenandoah"

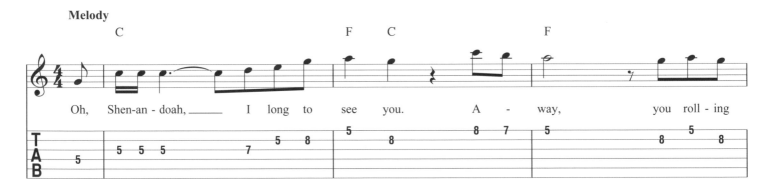

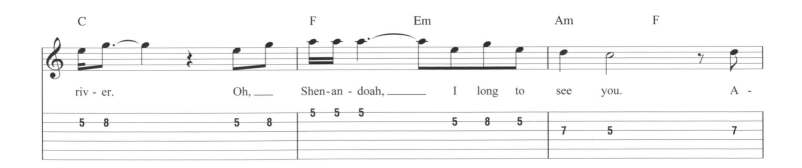

62

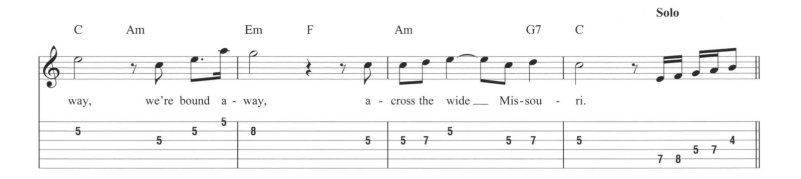

way,   we're bound a - way,   a - cross the wide ___ Mis-sou - ri.

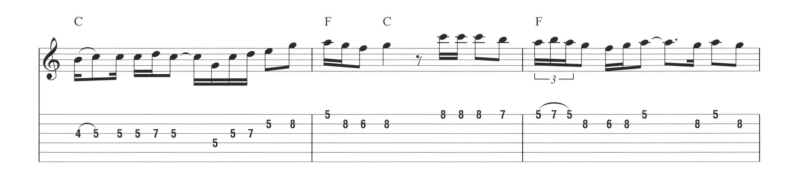

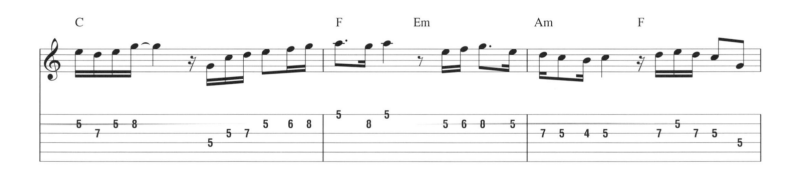

SWITCHING BASES

Some melodies have such a broad range (from low to high notes) that no single chord-based scale can encompass the whole tune. When this occurs, you have to switch in the middle of the tune, from a lower to a higher position or vice-versa. That's what happens in the following fiddle tune "Turkey in the Straw."

Fiddle tunes are a staple of the country, bluegrass, and old-time music genres, and they are excellent major scale exercises. "Turkey in the Straw," the nearly 200-year old tune, is a good example. Like most traditional fiddle tunes, it has an A section and a B section, each of which is played twice. In other words, AABB is "once around the tune." Like jazz standards, fiddle tunes often have traditional keys. "Turkey in the Straw" is usually played in the key of G, so you begin this arrangement in the D position at the seventh fret, and switch to the A position at the 12th fret for the B section.

 49. "Turkey in the Straw"

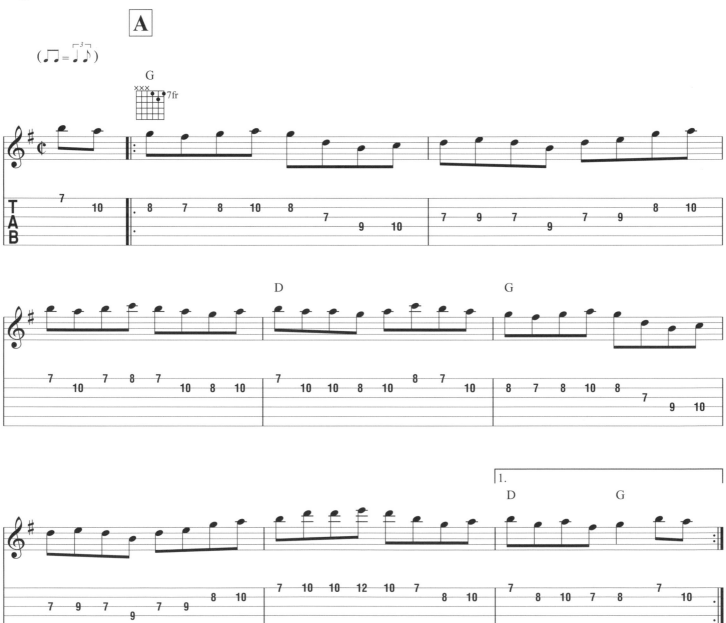

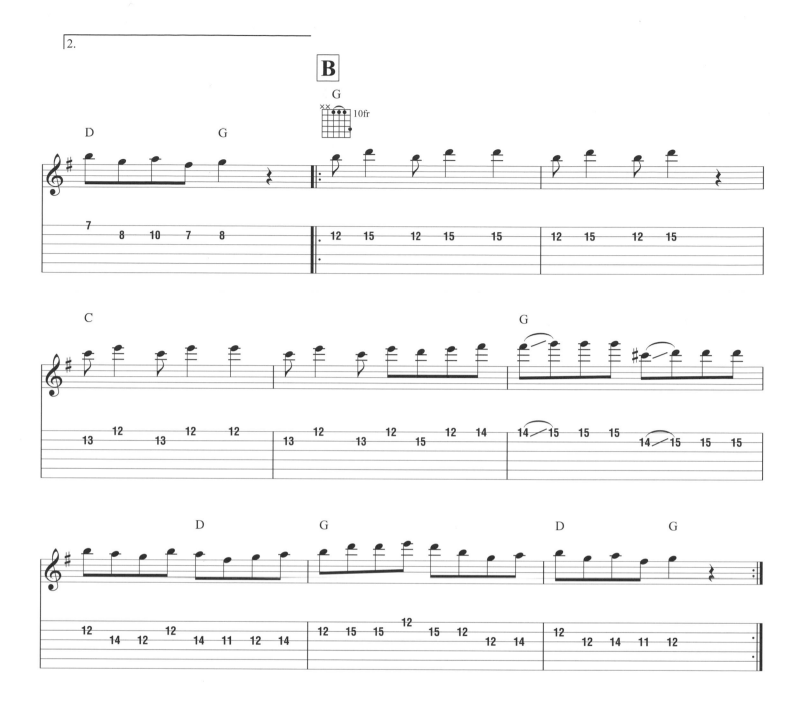

FOLLOWING THROUGH

Listen to more fiddle tunes and try playing them using both open-position and movable major scales. They make great warm-up exercises! Especially popular titles include "Arkansas Traveler," "Soldier's Joy," "Old Joe Clark," "Sally Gooden," "Blackberry Blossom," and "Cripple Creek."

Practice jamming with recordings or other players, using major scales on tunes that don't have bluesy melodies. There are many songs that fit that description in rock, pop, country, folk, R&B, and bluegrass.

JAILBREAK 8
Movable Major Pentatonic Scales

When solos based on minor pentatonic scales clash with a tune, the most popular scale-based strategy for lead guitarists becomes movable major pentatonic scales.

The major pentatonic scale that is favored by rock, pop, and country guitarists horizontally goes up the fretboard. It can start on the fifth- or sixth-string root notes, as shown here:

 50. C and G Major Pentatonic Scales

C Major Pentatonic Scale

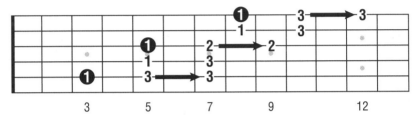

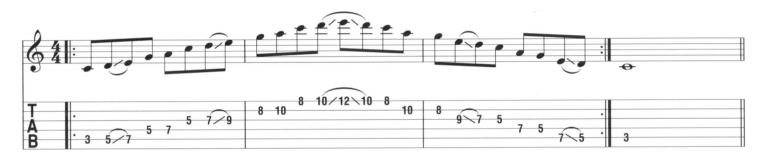

G Major Pentatonic Scale

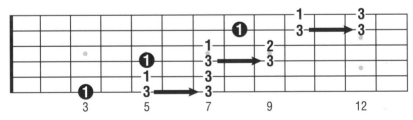

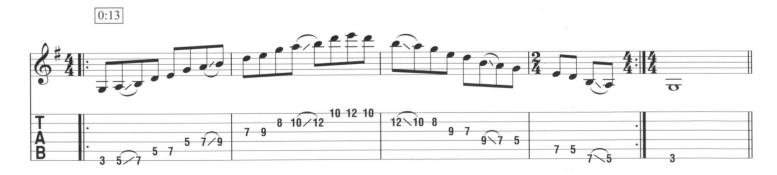

The two scales are almost identical in shape. Play them as written, going up and down each scale in a loop. Use the fingering that is indicated by the numbers on the fretboard; they make the scales flow easily and rapidly.

- These scales include *slides,* and the notes that slide up can also be bent with a bluesy effect.

- The scales are movable, and you locate them by playing the root note on the fifth or sixth string with your index finger. For example, if you start the sixth-string root scale at the first fret, it's an F major pentatonic scale.

BUILDING MAJOR PENTATONIC LICKS

You can build licks from these scales by circling around one area of the fretboard, like this:

 51. Major Pentatonic Licks

C Major Pentatonic Scale

Track 52, "Chilly Winds," appears on the next page to allow for easier reading.

If a song stays mostly within one chord family (using the I, IV, and V chords and their relative minors), you can use the major pentatonic scale that corresponds to the song's key throughout, as you did earlier with minor pentatonic scales. That's what happens in the following solo to the old folk song, "Chilly Winds," in the key of F. The first time around the tune, the melody is played with very little ornamentation. The second time around, the solo features typical major pentatonic frills and ad-libs.

 52. "Chilly Winds"

F Major Pentatonic Scale

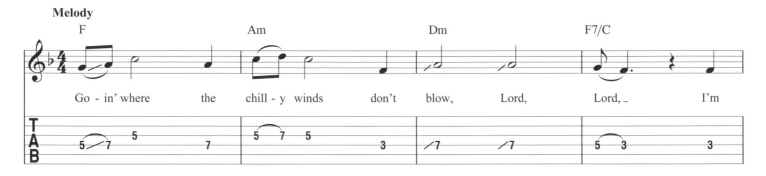

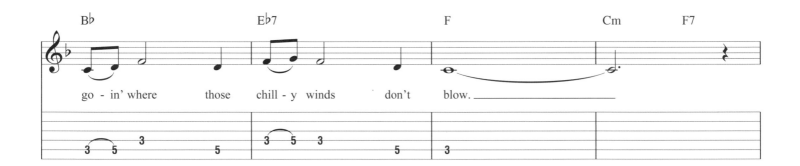

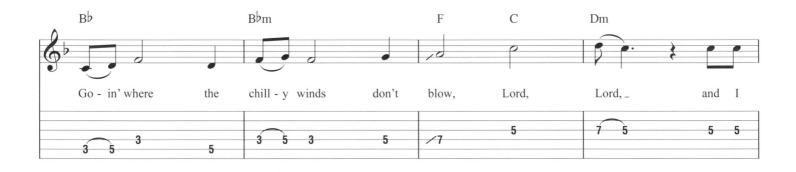

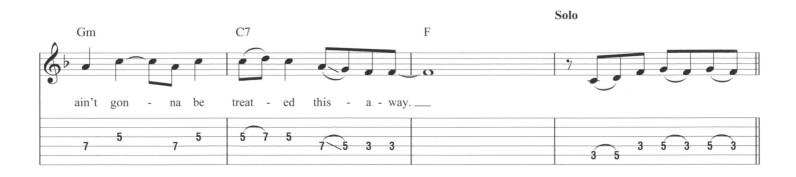

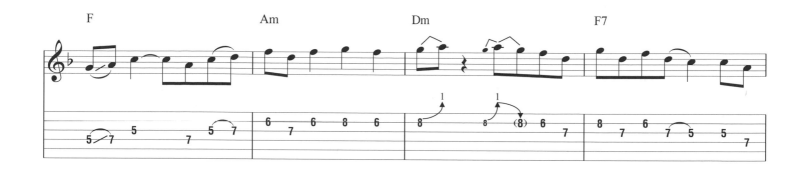

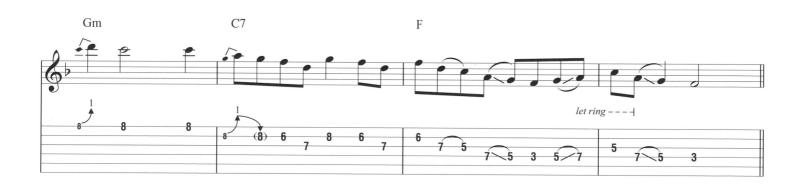

Instead of basing an entire solo on the scale of the I chord, you can also switch scales with the chord changes. For instance, in the key of C, solo with the C major pentatonic scale during the C chord, and switch to the G major pentatonic scale when the progression goes to a G chord. This is especially appropriate when a chord change lasts several bars. In the following version of the traditional folk ballad, "I Never Will Marry," the soloist switches scales with every chord change. As usual, the melody is stated, and then it's ornamented during the solo.

 53. "I Never Will Marry"

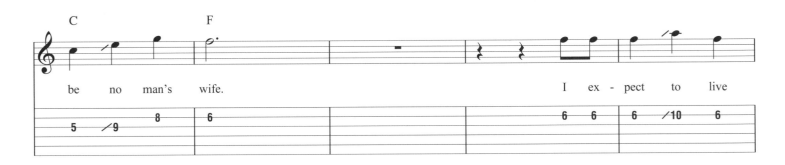

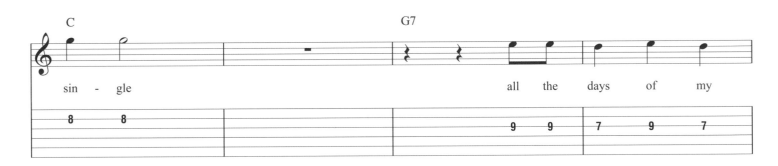

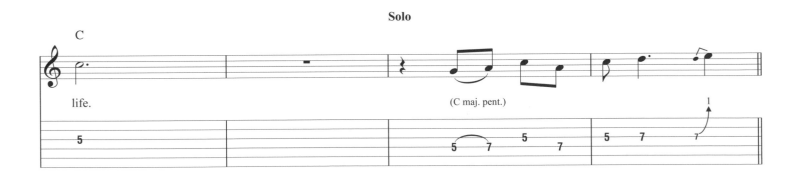

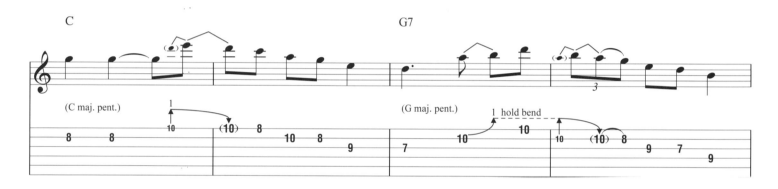

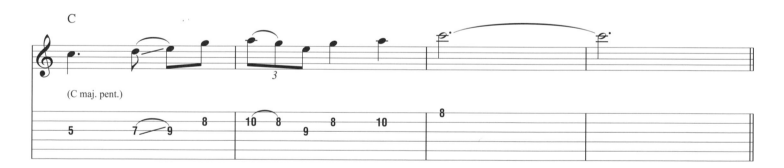

DOUBLE-STOP LICKS—SOUTHERN ROCK STYLE

Major pentatonic scales lend themselves to bluesy, double-stop licks that include string bending. This approach is especially popular in the Southern rock sounds of bands like Lynyrd Skynyrd and the Marshall Tucker Band. On the next page are some double-stop, string-bending licks derived from the major pentatonic scales.

54. G Licks and C Licks

G Licks

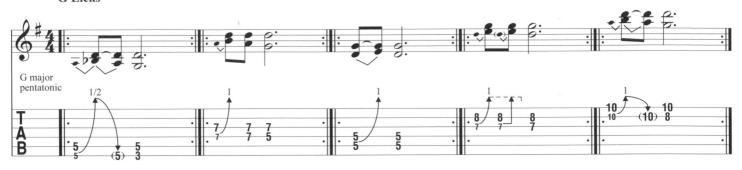

C Licks

The following solo to "Stagolee" makes use of these licks while expressing the song's melody:

 ## 55. "Stagolee"

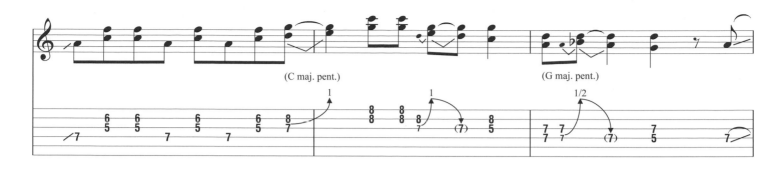

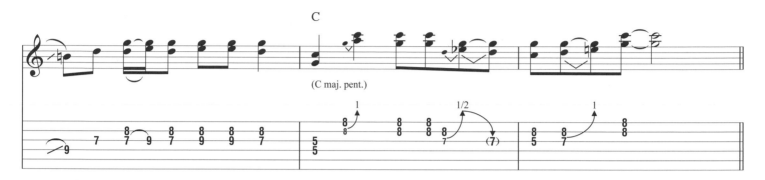

OPEN-POSITION E AND A MAJOR PENTATONIC SCALES

If you move the two major pentatonic scale patterns down below the nut, the sixth-string root pattern starts with the open E string, and the fifth-string root pattern starts on the open A string.

E Major Pentatonic

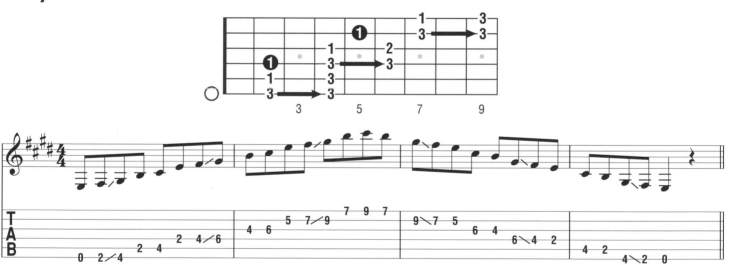

A Major Pentatonic

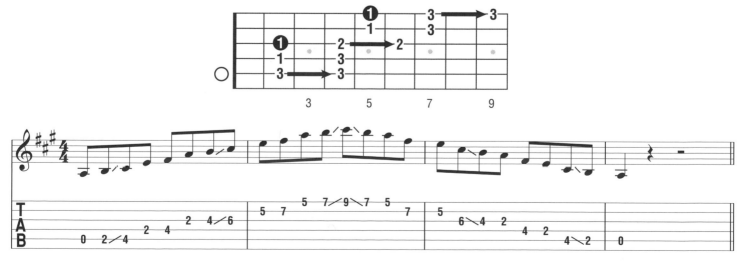

Many classic honky-tonk country licks come from these scale positions. Here's a sample. Note the slight mute on the open-A triplet that kicks off the tune as well as on the E-note triplet at the end of measure 4. This is a sample of the technique known as "chicken pickin'."

 56. "Honky-Tonk Heaven"

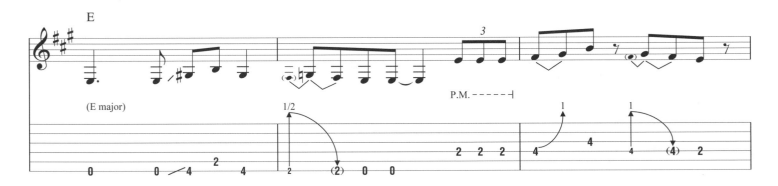

LISTENING SUGGESTIONS

Listen to classic country and honky-tonk tunes to hear some good examples of solos based on major pentatonic scales. Some classic rock tunes featuring textbook examples of soloing with major pentatonic scales include:

- "Ramblin' Man" by the Allman Brothers Band (Dickey Betts played the long solo in A♭; most of Betts' solos are based on the major pentatonic scale.)

- "Let It Be" by the Beatles (George Harrison playing solos in the key of C)

- "Maggie May" by Rod Stewart (Ron Wood playing solos in the key of D)

JAILBREAK 9
Solos Based on Movable Chord Shapes

Whether they play jazz, country, rock, bluegrass, or R&B, lead guitarists often base their solos on movable chords, rather than scales. For some reason, very little attention is paid to this soloing strategy in instructional guitar materials, while scales of all types are taught and discussed in detail. Yet nearly every accomplished lead guitarist plays both chord-based and scale-based solos, sometimes mixing both strategies in one solo. So if you only read and study one chapter in this book, make it this one!

You can play solos all over the fretboard, basing them on movable chord shapes. Just as you did in Chapter 1, you follow a song's chord progression and make up melodies, licks, and phrases from the notes in and around each chord. To do this, you'll have to learn several movable chord shapes and become familiar with the useful notes that surround each shape so you can invent licks or play melodies.

NOTES ON THE FIFTH AND SIXTH STRINGS

Once you start playing chords up the neck, it's helpful to know some notes on the fretboard. You don't have to know all of them, but learn the notes on the sixth and fifth strings. Note that at the 12th fret, the pattern repeats itself.

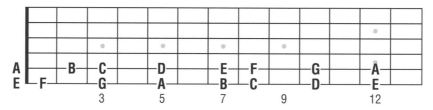

SOME MOVABLE SHAPES

Start with the old cowboy ballad, "Red River Valley." This version is in the key of D and uses three chord shapes: the A shape, which is the open-position A chord made movable, the F shape, and the F7 shape.

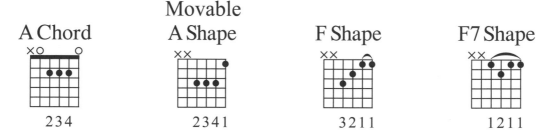

You can play these chords all over the fretboard, if you know their root notes. For example, the root note of the F and F7 shapes is located on the first string, which is the same note as the sixth string.

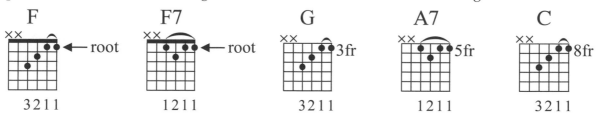

The root note of the A shape is on the third string. You can use the fifth string to place it on the fretboard once you realize that this is a variation of the A-shape barre chord.

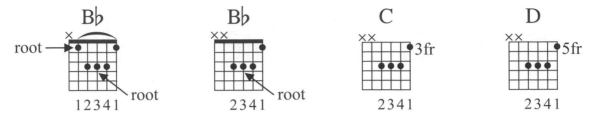

Each of these shapes can be played all over the fretboard, as they contain no open strings. In "Red River Valley," they are played like this:

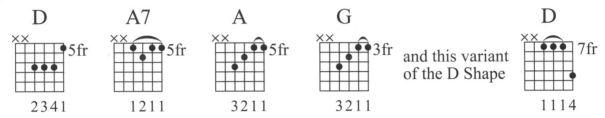

and this variant
of the D Shape

ADDING THE ADJACENT NOTES

Next, you need to know the useful notes that are adjacent to these shapes. In the diagrams below, the filled circles are the chord tones, open circles are scale tones, and the diamonds indicate blue notes. (You can see them at work in Example 57.)

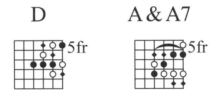

 57. Chord-Based Licks in Country Music

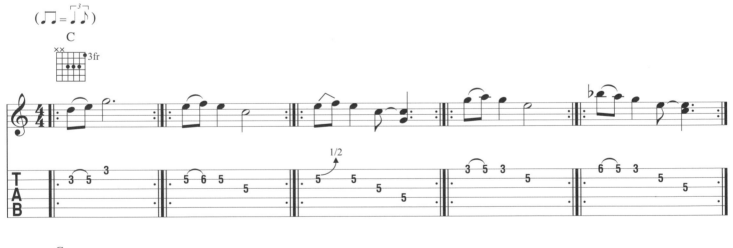

Here's the basic melody to "Red River Valley," followed by a Willie Nelson-style, chord-based country solo. Note that you don't have to hold each chord position while playing licks based on that position. Instead, your hand should hover over the chord shape and use it as a frame of reference.

 58. **"Red River Valley"**

R&B AND ROCK CHORD STYLES

In the early 1960s, R&B guitarists like Curtis Mayfield and Cornell Dupree developed a chord-based soloing style which in turn influenced Jimi Hendrix, John Frusciante (Red Hot Chili Peppers), and other rock and soul players. Here are some chord shapes that can be used to create chord-based licks and solos in the style of these legendary guitarists. Learn these well, as you'll be playing them in an R&B-flavored version of "Greensleeves" shortly.

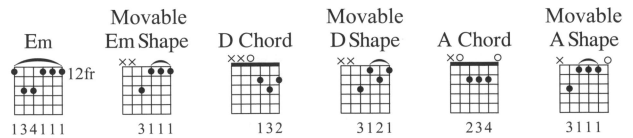

Here are the useful notes that are adjacent to these shapes:

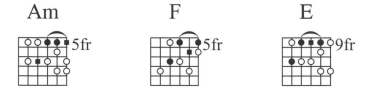

Now here are some licks to learn from these chords.

 ## 59. More Chord-Based Licks

The following solo to "Greensleeves" makes use of the shapes and licks you just learned.

60. "Greensleeves"

Melody

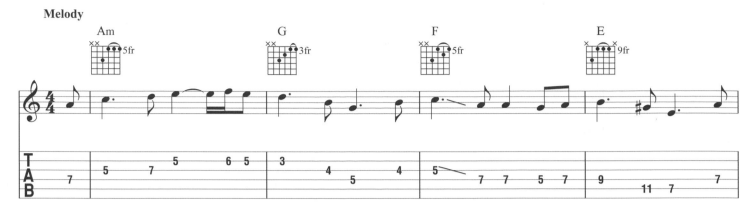

Solo

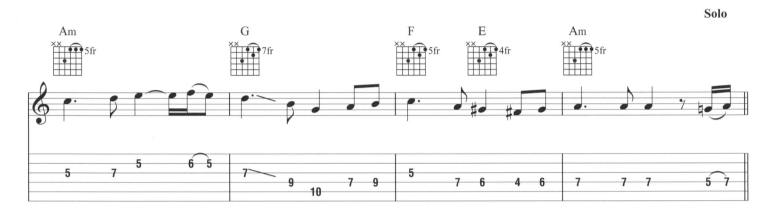

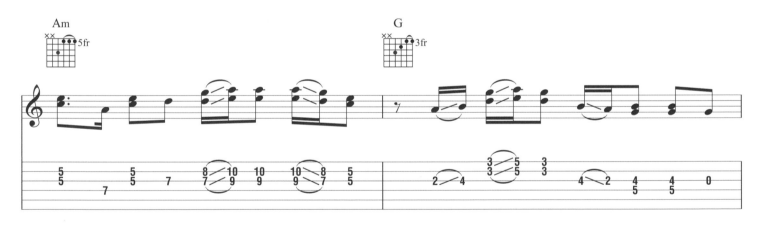

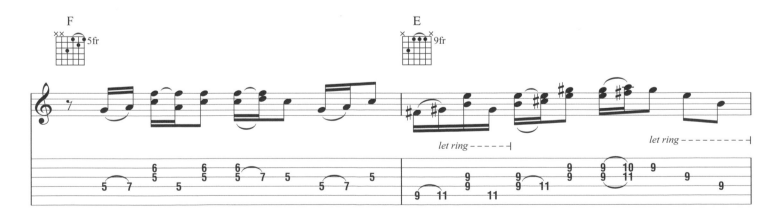

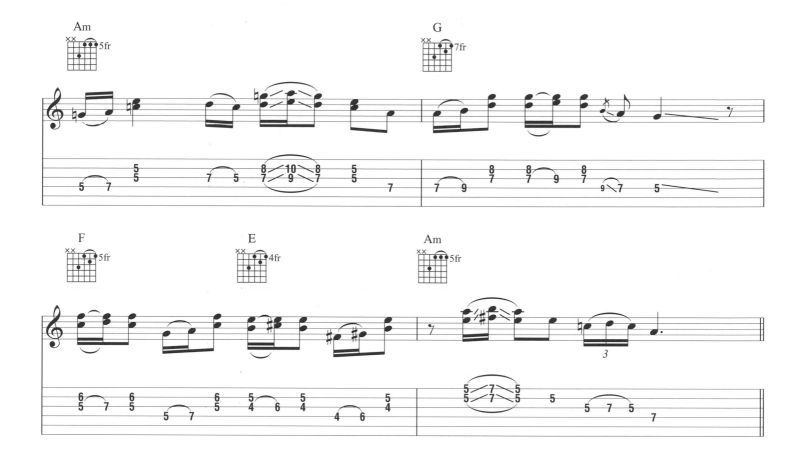

CHORD-BASED JAZZ SOLOING

Jazz solos are often based on chord shapes. In fact, many legendary jazz guitarists are famous for playing *chord-melody style,* a pianistic technique in which you play chords and melody at the same time. To do this, you need to know many chord shapes and several ways to play any given chord.

The chord-melody solo that follows for the jazz standard "Poor Butterfly" is a good example of the style. Before attempting to play this arrangement, listen to the track to become familiar with the melody, and strum the chords with or without the track to become familiar with some new shapes. Many of the chords you'll encounter are slight variations of chord shapes you've already played.

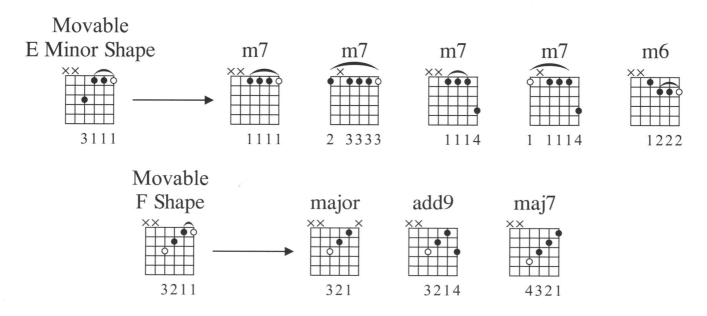

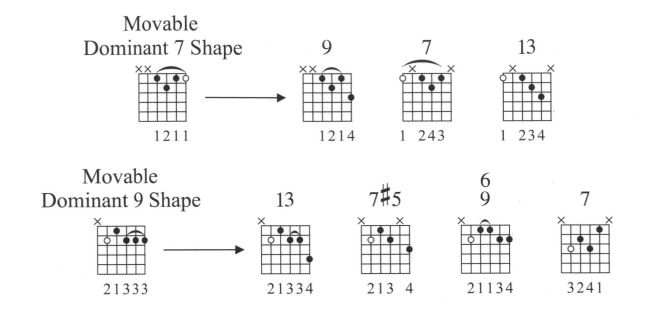

"Poor Butterfly" has been recorded by countless jazz singers and instrumentalists. Instrumental versions of the song—including the one below—are played usually in the key of A♭. You can play any song in any key, but jazz instrumentalists usually play in the key in which the song was composed.

61. "Poor Butterfly" (Chord-Melody Style)

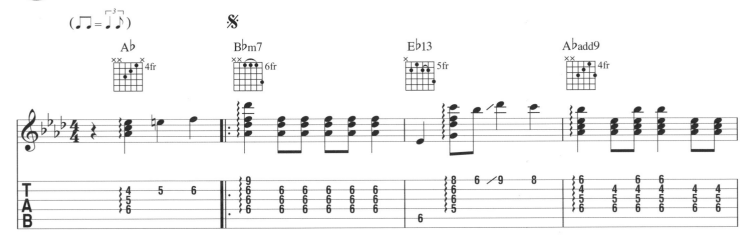

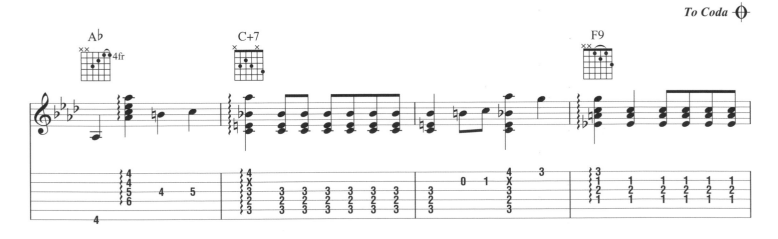

You can create a single-note solo to "Poor Butterfly" using the same shapes you used in the chord-melody version. You've already looked at the useful notes that are adjacent to some of these shapes (F, F7, movable Em). Now, if you study the notes and licks that go with the 9th shape here, you'll be ready to invent single-note solos for "Poor Butterfly."

62. Ninth Chord-Shape Licks

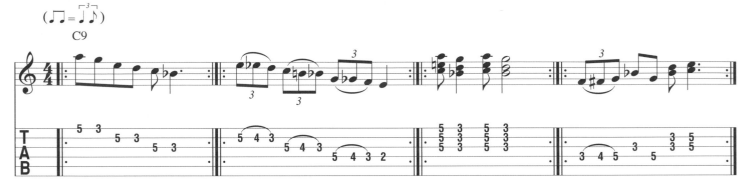

Alright, give this single-note solo for "Poor Butterfly" a shot:

63. "Poor Butterfly" (Single-Note Solo)

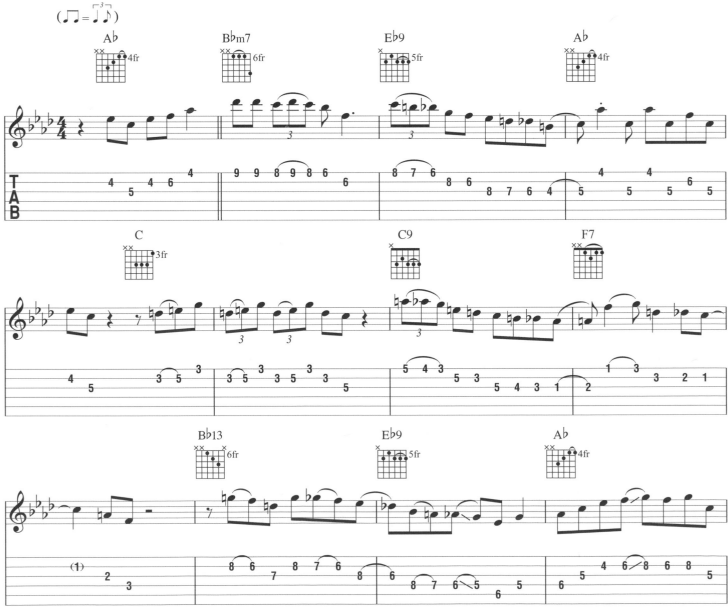

LISTENING SUGGESTIONS

For country solos that are chord-based, listen to Willie Nelson's "Blue Eyes Crying in the Rain," as well as his other solos. Also, check out the solos of James Burton (who backed up Elvis Presley, Emmylou Harris, and many others) or Ricky Skaggs.

For R&B and rock solos, listen to Jimi Hendrix ballads like "Little Wing," "The Wind Cries Mary," and "Castles Made of Sand." Also, give Curtis Mayfield's "People Get Ready" and the Red Hot Chili Peppers' "Under the Bridge" a listen.

For jazz chord-melody playing and single-note playing, listen to Joe Pass, Barney Kessel, Kenny Burrell, and Tal Farlow.

To become adept at chord-based soloing, you need to know how to play many chord shapes, especially movable ones, and you need to know many ways to play any given chord in high, low, and medium registers. *Fretboard Roadmaps for Guitar* by Fred Sokolow (Hal Leonard) shows how to do this in great detail.

AFTERWORD

As you practice the soloing approaches in the preceding chapters, you'll feel the prison bars of the scale-jail melting away. You'll have multiple strategies for soloing—some based on scales, some based on chords. Familiarity with these techniques is liberating; given a soloing opportunity, you have many possible choices and many skills at hand. You can mix up the different licks and styles as they occur to you or stick to one particular approach. You have freedom of movement!

Best of all, once you are familiar with the various scale-based and chord-based ideas, your fingers know where the notes are and you can play *intentionally*, instead of being confined to a repetitious pattern—the very definition of scale-jail. With this newfound and hard-earned knowledge, you can play whatever licks, phrases, or melodies occur to you. Now you're really *playing* guitar, and you're free at last!

ABOUT THE AUTHOR

Fred Sokolow is best-known as the author of over 150 instructional and transcription books and video materials for guitar, banjo, Dobro, mandolin, lap steel, autoharp, and ukulele. Fred has long been a well-known West Coast multi-string instrument performer and recording artist, particularly on the acoustic music scene. The diverse musical genres covered in his books and video materials, along with several bluegrass, jazz, and rock recordings that he has released, demonstrate his mastery of many musical styles. Whether he's playing Delta bottleneck blues, bluegrass, old-time banjo, '30s swing guitar, or screaming rock solos, he does it with authenticity and passion.

Other books from Fred that may be of interest:

Basic Blues for Guitar (book/audio), Hal Leonard

Basic Fingerpicking: A Guide to Fingerpicking in All Styles (book/audio), Hal Leonard

Hal Leonard Bluegrass Guitar Method (book/audio), Hal Leonard

Building a Jazz Chord Solo (book/audio), Hal Leonard

Dictionary of Strums and Picking Patterns (book/audio), Hal Leonard

Hal Leonard Folk Guitar Method (book/audio), Hal Leonard

Fretboard Roadmaps for Acoustic Guitar (book/audio), Hal Leonard

Fretboard Roadmaps for Bluegrass and Folk Guitar (book/audio), Hal Leonard

Fretboard Roadmaps for Blues Guitar (book/audio), Hal Leonard

Fretboard Roadmaps for Country Guitar (book/audio), Hal Leonard

Fretboard Roadmaps for Guitar, Second Edition (book/audio), Hal Leonard

Fretboard Roadmaps for Jazz Guitar (book/audio), Hal Leonard

Jazzing It Up (book/audio), Hal Leonard

Rockabilly Guitar Method (book/audio), Hal Leonard

Shortcuts for Guitar (book/audio), Hal Leonard

Western Swing Guitar (book), Hal Leonard